HERBS &

AN ILLUSTRATED GUIDE TO OVER 120 HERBS & SPICES

SPICES

JILL NORMAN

Photography
Dave King

METRO BOOKS
New York

METRO BOOKS
New York

An Imprint of Sterling Publishing
387 Park Avenue South
New York, NY 10016

METRO BOOKS and the distinctive Metro Books logo
are trademarks of Sterling Publishing Co., Inc

For Paul, who made it possible

This edition
Jacket Design Mark Penfound
Special Sales Creative Project Manager Alison Donovan
DTP Designer Satish Chandra Gaur
Senior DTP Designer Pushpak Tyagi
Pre-Production Producer Sarah Isle
Pre-Production Manager Sunil Sharma
Producer Verity Powell

Original 2002 edition
Project Editor Frank Ritter
Editor Hugh Thompson
Project Art Editor Toni Kay
Art Editor Sara Robin
Managing Editor Gillian Roberts
US Editor Norma MacMillan
Art Director Carole Ash
Category Publisher Mary-Clare Jerram
DTP Designers Sonia Charbonnier, Louise Waller
Production Controller Joanna Bull

ISBN 978-1-4351-5201-4

A catalog record for this book is available from the
Library of Congress.

For information about custom editions, special sales,
and premium and corporate purchases, please contact
Sterling Special Sales at 800-805-5489 or
specialsales@sterlingpublishing.com.

Manufactured in China

2 4 6 8 10 9 7 5 3 1

www.sterlingpublishing.com

CONTENTS

Introduction 6

What defines an herb or spice, and why are they used in
cooking? Regional cuisines derive much of their character
from how specific herbs and spices are combined and used.
With increasing availability of fresh herbs and spices from around
the world, every cook can recreate authentic regional dishes at
home, and try out new combinations to his or her personal taste.

Herbs

Introducing herbs 8

While robust herbs such as sage do not lose their flavors if
dried, most herbs are meant to be eaten fresh. Herbs added
at the beginning of cooking impart their flavor to foods; adding
the herbs at the end ensures that their aroma is retained. In this
directory, more than 60 herbs and their varieties are grouped
by aroma and taste.

Spices

Introducing spices   84
Most spice plants are native to the Asian tropics and were
used in cooking long before European powers fought for control
of their trade. Traditionally many spices have been combined
with others, and mixtures vary according to the dish and the
cook. The directory of spices contains more than 60 spices
and their variants, each placed in a family of taste and
aroma. It is explained how the spices are used worldwide,
which herbs and spices combine well, and which foods best
complement each spice.

Simple, reliable descriptions of the techniques you
need to get the best from every spice.

The definition of what constitutes an herb or spice is not as straightforward as it might seem. Broadly, we think of herbs as plants used by cooks for their flavor and aroma. The word herb derives from the Latin *herba*, meaning grass or, by extension, green crop: it was originally applied to a wide range of leaf vegetables in addition to the plants we now call herbs. Most of the culinary herbs we use grow in temperate climates. Spices, on the other hand, are products of tropical plants: aromatic roots, bark, seeds, buds, and fruits, usually used in dried form, whether whole or ground. Again our word derives from Latin, where *species* meant specific kind but, in later use, goods or merchandise – spices certainly being an important commodity even at the time of the Romans.

How the book is organized

I have followed standard European usage in defining herbs and spices, and have grouped both according to their dominant aroma and flavor. Some fitted easily into a specific category; others were difficult to define and could have been put into more than one group. Marigolds, for instance, are basically sweet, yet have a bitter note. Some Asian basils are more piquant than sweet. Ginger is pungent but it is also earthy and warm. Another difficulty is that the way we express our awareness of flavors and aromas varies from individual to individual. Your perception of aromatics may not be the same as mine, and a different term may come to your mind from the one that came to mine.

The American Spice Trade Association defines "any dried plant used primarily for seasoning purposes" as a spice; this includes dried herbs, even dehydrated onions. In Southeast Asia, any aromatic plant used fresh is an herb, but once the same substance is dried it is classed as a spice. I have followed European usage and classed all herbs as herbs and all spices as spices, whether fresh or dried.

Health benefits of herbs and spices

The early use of herbs and spices was medicinal, and in many regions where they grow they are still valued for their medicinal properties. Often their use in cooking owed as much to their perceived ability to promote health, combat flatulence, or help digest fatty foods as to their appetizing fragrances. Fresh herbs and spices provided mineral salts and vitamins long before our need for these was understood. In tropical countries the vitamin C contained in chili peppers remains just as important to the diet as the lift that the chilies give to it.

Most cultures recognize the importance of providing a balance in food. Indian cooking follows Ayurvedic principles in using herbs and spices to provide flavor and to create physical and emotional wellbeing. In China, nutrition and medicine have long been integrated. Chinese cooking is based on a theory that wellbeing is brought about by the careful balancing of the five flavors – sweet, salty, bitter, sour, and pungent – with the texture and color of the food. Yin herbs such as mint and parsley slow down the metabolism, whereas yang spices such as chili and ginger activate it. Similar principles are followed in Iran, where the cook strives to maintain a balance between ingredients classed as hot or cold. In the West, herbs and spices have become important elements in adding flavor to low-salt and low-fat foods; and garlic has gained wider acceptance because it is said to lower cholesterol levels and help prevent heart disease.

Flavorings rooted in tradition

In the past herbs and spices were also important for their preservative properties: before the arrival of refrigeration their volatile oils and other compounds prolonged the useful life of many foodstuffs. Pickled or salted meat, fish, and vegetables would last through the winter months, and aromatics were used to improve their flavor. Although we no longer need these methods of preserving, we still use many of them simply because we have come to like the taste they impart to foods.

Herbs and spices are used to stimulate all the senses, not just the tastebuds, through their aroma, flavor, texture, and visual appeal. In all the regions of the world, traditional flavor combinations, using local ingredients, have come to characterize the foods of those regions. Saffron, pimentón, garlic, and nuts dominate in Spain; wine and herbs in France; basil, garlic, olive oil, and anchovy in Italy. In Britain, it is parsley, thyme, sage, and mustard; in eastern Europe, sour cream, dill, and caraway. The Middle East uses lemon, parsley, and cinnamon. In northern India, ginger, garlic, and cumin are the most important spices; in southern India, it is mustard seed, coconut, chili, and tamarind. Thailand has fish sauce, lemon grass, galangal, and chili; in China, it is soy sauce, ginger, and Sichuan pepper. Mexico remains faithful to its chilies, cilantro, and cinnamon.

We are becoming increasingly aware of these traditional patterns as the demand for and availability of authentic ethnic food grows. The number of herbs offered in stores and markets, and of spices and spice mixtures sold in supermarkets and specialty stores, has dramatically increased, as has the number of forms in which herbs and spices are now marketed. Herbs preserved in oil or freeze-dried are now readily available, as are organic herbs and spices and ever more spice blends. We are becoming more knowledgeable, and more adventurous.

Herb and spice combinations

This leads me to end on a note of caution. Herbs and spices should not be overused, and only their skillful blending leads to a successful dish. Just as too much of a specific herb or spice can ruin a dish, flavors in herb and spice mixtures can cancel each other out. Experiment with combinations you think you will like, but do so with caution; you will find that herbs and spices can bring subtlety, harmony, and complexity to your cooking.

Jill Norman

herbs

While compiling the herb directory in this book I became conscious of the impact of world trade expansion on the sale of fresh herbs. It has long been accepted that spices, and to a lesser extent dried herbs, can travel great distances without damage, and in recent years air freight has also made it possible to import fresh spices, such as ginger, lemon grass, chili peppers, and zedoary (white turmeric). But herbs were always considered too fragile for long transportation; when I last wrote about herbs some five or six years ago it was almost impossible to find some Asian basils, or Japanese herbs such as perilla or mitsuba.

Today international trade brings herbs grown in Turkey, Cyprus, and Israel to my supermarket shelves as a matter of course. Deliveries from Japan, Thailand, and Singapore bring little-known tropical herbs at least once a week to specialty stores. At present, demand probably comes largely from immigrant communities and from restaurants, but my own visits to such markets revealed a great curiosity and a willingness to experiment on the part of other local enthusiasts. With these people in mind I have included a number of recent arrivals. In the US, and in other countries with sufficiently warm climates, many herbs are already being cultivated to meet demand not just from immigrants but also, increasingly, from a wider public.

The Western tradition

Many herbs remain essential in classic European cuisines: tarragon, thyme, bay, and garlic in France; basil, sage, and rosemary in Italy; oregano in Greece; dill in

Scandinavia; parsley, sage, thyme, and bay in Britain. The traditional uses of these herbs are still reflected in the choices made by today's cooks, but the foods with which they are used and their flavor combinations are changing as other possibilities, afforded as much by our own curiosity as by increased availability, are explored. If you are a novice in cooking with herbs, start with classics such as chicken with tarragon, guacamole with cilantro and chili, grilled cod or tuna with salsa verde, roast potatoes with rosemary and garlic, or a beef stew with a bouquet garni and red wine. Once you begin to appreciate how the blending of flavors affects a dish, you will be drawn to experiment and adapt or devise combinations to your own taste.

We are rediscovering many herbs that once were in common use but have long been forgotten or neglected as weeds. In 17th-century Europe, salad herbs were grown and used widely. In 1699, John Evelyn's *Acetaria* recorded more than 30 salad herbs, including arugula, basil, balm, chicory, corn salad, clary sage, various cresses, dandelion, fennel, hyssop, mallow, mint, orach, purslane, and sorrel. In 1731, Philip Miller's *Gardener's Dictionary* instructed gentlemen gardeners in herb cultivation. Some have become easily available once more, in season and even all year round, but others – such as sweet cicely, clary sage, and hyssop – you will have to grow yourself. Specialist nurseries are constantly extending their stocks to meet the demand for a wider range of herbs.

Choosing and using herbs

Generally, herbs are used to add fragrance and flavor rather than to provide the dominant taste. The light flavors of dill, parsley, and chervil are good with fish and seafood; the more pungent rosemary, oregano, and garlic will flavor braised or baked lamb or roast pork beautifully. Root vegetables respond well to thyme and rosemary, eggplant to Provençal herbs, green peas to chives, tomatoes to basil and parsley. It is important always to balance delicate and hearty flavors, and to use herbs judiciously.

The wealth of fresh herbs now available has had the beneficial effect of banishing from many kitchens a lot of small packets of stale dried herbs. Some herbs that are

ROSEMARY   FLAT-LEAF PARSLEY   BASIL   GARLIC

sold dried, such as basil and parsley, are never worth having; their aroma is musty
at best, and their taste insipid. Such herbs are meant to be eaten fresh. The clean,
herbaceous notes of fresh parsley, and the complex, sweet scent of anise and clove
wafting from a bunch of basil, beguile first the sense of smell and later also the
tastebuds. Unlike many herbs, these two are not overwhelming if used in large quantities
– as they are in the basil sauce pesto and the parsley salad tabbouleh. Robust herbs,
such as oregano, thyme, sage, savory, mint, and rosemary, respond well to drying,
which preserves and often concentrates their flavor. Whether fresh or dried, these herbs
should be used sparingly or they will overwhelm other flavors in the food instead of
complementing them.

Herbs added early on in cooking will release their flavors into the dish. Dried herbs
should always be put in at the beginning, and herbs with tough leaves, such as rosemary,
lavender, winter savory, thyme, and bay, will withstand long cooking. If you add sprigs
of herbs to a dish, remove them before serving. To restore the aroma of herbs used in
a slow-cooked dish, stir a few finely chopped leaves into the pan toward the end of the
cooking process. Strongly flavored herbs, such as mint, tarragon, fennel, marjoram, and
lovage, can be added at any stage during cooking. The essential oils of delicate herbs, like
basil, chervil, chives, dill, cilantro, perilla, and lemon balm, soon dissipate when heated.
To keep them fresh in taste, texture, and color, add them just before a dish is served.

PARSLEY
Petroselinum crispum

Probably the only herb considered indispensable by most Western cooks, parsley is a truly versatile biennial, native to the eastern Mediterranean region. Today it is cultivated throughout most of the temperate world. Parsley root, which is valued for its root rather than its leaves, was first grown in Germany in the 16th century.

Culinary uses

Parsley is liked for its clean, fresh taste and is rich in iron and vitamins A and C. It is used in sauces, salads, stuffings, and omelettes in many parts of the world. In Anglo-Saxon cultures its use as a flavoring ingredient (except in a parsley sauce) rather than simply as a garnish is quite recent. Add chopped parsley at the end of cooking time for a fresh flavor. Sprigs of dark green, deep-fried curly parsley make an excellent garnish for fried fish. Parsley root is used in soups and stews, but it can also be blanched and then roasted or cooked in other ways as a root vegetable. It mashes well with potato.

Essential to a number of traditional flavoring mixtures: French bouquets garnis, fines herbes, and persillade; Italian gremolata and salsa verde; and tabbouleh.

Good with eggs, fish, lemon, lentils, rice, tomatoes, most vegetables.

Combines well with basil, bay, capers, chervil, chili, chives, garlic, lemon balm, marjoram, mint, oregano, pepper, rosemary, sorrel, sumac, tarragon.

Curly parsley *P. crispum*
Good for garnishes, curly parsley also gives a light, herbaceous flavor and attractive green color to mayonnaise and other sauces.

Flat-leaf parsley
P. c. var. 'Neapolitanum'

Also called French or Italian parsley, flat-leaf parsley has the best flavor for cooking, and is most widely used throughout Europe and the Middle East.

STEMS
Parsley stems are coarser in flavor than the leaves. Tie them in a bundle and use in long-cooked stocks and stews; discard the stems when the cooking is finished.

Parsley root
P. c. var. *tuberosum*

Mostly cultivated in central and northern Europe, parsley root, also called Hamburg parsley, is no more difficult to grow than leaf parsley. It looks like a small parsnip or, if round, a turnip. Its flavor combines those of parsley and celery, with a light nuttiness. The leaves have a coarse flavor and texture.

fresh and mild herbs

PURSLANE

Portulaca oleracea

Purslane is a sprawling annual that grows wild throughout much of the world. It has been used as a food plant for centuries in southern Europe and the Middle East. An important source of iron and vitamin C, purslane is also one of the best plant sources of Omega-3, one of the fatty acids that help to maintain a healthy heart.

Culinary uses

Young leaves make an agreeable addition to a salad. In the Middle East, chopped purslane with a garlicky yogurt dressing is served as an accompaniment to grilled meats. The herb is also a standard ingredient of fattoush, the Lebanese salad.

Blanch older leaves to use as a vegetable. Cooking emphasizes their mucilaginous content, which provides a good thickening for soups and stews. In Turkey, large bunches of purslane are used in a traditional lamb and bean stew, and all around the Mediterranean it turns up in soups. The Mexicans cook it with pork, tomatillos, and chili peppers, especially smoky chipotles (*p.173*). Purslane combines well with spinach tossed in olive oil and lemon juice.

Good with beets, cucumber, eggs, fava beans, feta cheese, new potatoes, spinach, tomatoes, yogurt.

Combines well with arugula, borage, chervil, cresses, salad burnet, sorrel.

Fresh sprigs and flowers

Green purslane has oblong, thick, succulent leaves and a round stem tinged with red. Golden purslane (*P. sativa*) is a smaller plant and is less hardy.

MINER'S LETTUCE
Claytonia perfoliata

Miner's lettuce, also called claytonia and winter purslane, is a
delicate-looking annual that makes an excellent winter salad herb.
It is called miner's lettuce because miners in the California Gold Rush
ate the wild plant to avoid scurvy – like the unrelated purslane
Portulaca oleracea (p.14), miner's lettuce is high in vitamin C.

Culinary uses

Leaves, young stems, and flowers make
a useful and pretty contribution to the
salad bowl. I particularly like miner's
lettuce for its winter usefulness, when
other salad greens can be dreary.

The leaves and stems can be cooked –
try them alone or with other greens,
stir-fried with a little oyster sauce.
Combines well with arugula, chives,
sorrel, watercress.

PARTS USED

Leaves, young stems,
and flowers.

BUYING AND STORING

Miner's lettuce can be
gathered from the wild in
shady grasslands in North
America, its native habitat,
but it is less commonly
found in Europe. It is best
picked and used at once,
but can be kept in a plastic
bag in the refrigerator for
1–2 days.

Fresh sprigs and flowers

Miner's lettuce leaves totally encircle the
smooth stems. The tiny, white flowers are
borne on thin stems from early summer.

GROW YOUR OWN

A few herb nurseries now
stock miner's lettuce, but
it is also easy to grow from
seed. Seeds sown in spring
will produce plants for
summer use; summer
sowing will produce plants
for winter picking. Miner's
lettuce does survive near-
freezing temperatures. It
prefers a light soil, but is
adaptable. Miner's lettuce
makes a pretty garden
edging plant.

BORAGE

Borago officinalis

This robust, annual herb, native to southern Europe and western Asia, is now naturalized throughout Europe and North America. It is worth growing just for its dazzling, blue, star-like flowers. The old herbalists held that borage made people cheerful and courageous; it is now known to stimulate the adrenal glands and have mild sedative and antidepressant effects.

PARTS USED

Leaves and flowers.
Avoid the bristly stems.

BUYING AND STORING

Borage is always used fresh. Leaves can be kept for a day or two in the vegetable crisper of the refrigerator, either wrapped in damp paper towel or placed inside a plastic bag. Flowers are best used soon after picking or they will wilt. Freeze them in ice cubes and serve in drinks.

GROW YOUR OWN

Grow borage in well-drained soil in a sunny spot. It is a large, ungainly plant and will self-seed easily. Plant borage only where you intend it to grow because it has a long taproot and does not like to be moved. Harvest young leaves in spring and summer, and pick the flowers as soon as they open.

Culinary uses

Borage is essentially a salad herb. Shred the young leaves, because their hairy texture is disagreeable if they are left whole. Combine the shredded leaves with cucumber tossed in yogurt or sour cream, and add them to dressings and salsas. Tough older leaves can be sautéed, or cooked in water and treated like spinach. The Italians use borage with spinach or with bread crumbs, egg, and Parmesan cheese to stuff ravioli and cannelloni. The Turks add the leaves to green pea soup. The flowers will impart a delicate cucumber note to salads, and they look wonderful floating on a creamy soup or flavoring a summer punch. They can also be candied to decorate cakes and desserts. Use borage sparingly.
Good with eel and other fatty fish, potato salad, white cheeses, yogurt; Pimm's and other summer punches.
Combines well with arugula, chervil, cresses, dill, garlic, mint, salad burnet.

Fresh leaves and flowers

Of borage species, only *B. officinalis* is edible. The white-flowered cultivated variety *B. o.* 'Alba' can be used in the same way as the blue- or purple-flowered varieties.

SALAD BURNET
Sanguisorba minor

Salad burnet is a graceful, bushy, perennial plant with sharply toothed, deep-green leaves. Although delicate in appearance, it is actually sturdy, its evergreen leaves often pushing up through a light covering of snow. Native to Europe and western Asia, salad burnet was taken to North America by early European colonists and is now naturalized there.

Culinary uses

The subtle flavor of the young, feathery leaves is best appreciated by eating them raw. Add them to salads – they are particularly good in autumn and winter, when interesting salad leaves can be in short supply. Chop as a garnish for vegetables or egg dishes; combine with tarragon, chives, and chervil for fines herbes. The leaves are good scattered over soups and casseroles, and made into sauces and herb butters. Burnet is often recommended to flavor vinegar, but I have found this disappointing.
Good with cream cheese, cucumber, eggs, fava beans, fish, salad leaves, tomatoes.
Combines well with chervil, chives, miner's lettuce, mint, parsley, rosemary, tarragon.

Fresh sprigs
The tender, young leaves have the best flavor. The pretty red flowers have no taste.

PERILLA
Perilla frutescens

The aromatic leaves of perilla – or shiso, to give the plant its Japanese name – are widely used in Japan, Korea, and Vietnam. More recently they have been discovered by cooks in Australia, the US, and Europe. An annual herb, related to mint and basil, perilla is native to China. The flavor of dried perilla only palely reflects that of the fresh.

Culinary uses

In Japan, red perilla is mostly used for coloring and pickling umeboshi (salted and dried "plums"). Green perilla is served with sushi and sashimi – it is said to counteract parasites in raw fish. The leaves are also used in soups and salads and to wrap rice cakes. Coated with batter on one side only, they are deep-fried for tempura. The Vietnamese shred perilla and add it to noodles; they serve grilled meat, shrimp, and fish wrapped in green perilla leaves with a spicy dipping sauce; and they also use it in salads.

Good with beef, chicken, fish, mooli, noodles and pasta, potatoes, rice, tomatoes, zucchini.

Combines well with basil, chives, fresh and pickled ginger, lemon grass, mitsuba, parsley, sansho, wasabi.

Green perilla *P. frutescens*

Green perilla has soft, downy leaves with a crinkly edge. They look somewhat like stinging nettle leaves.

MITSUBA
Cryptotaenia japonica

Mitsuba is also known as Japanese parsley, Japanese chervil, and trefoil. This cool-climate, elegant perennial grows wild in Japan and is used extensively in Japanese cooking. It is now cultivated in Australia, North America, and Europe, initially to supply Japanese restaurants but increasingly to sell to herb enthusiasts.

Culinary uses

In Japan, mitsuba is used to season soups, simmered dishes (nabemono), and savory custards, in salads, and with fried or vinegared foods. It adds its highly individual, delicate flavor to matsutake no dobinmushi, a dish made only for a few weeks when the much-prized pine mushrooms are in season. The mushrooms are simmered in a broth and the mitsuba is added for a few seconds at the end. Small bundles of stems can be tied in a knot below the leaves and fried for tempura. Mitsuba is often blanched quickly to tenderize the leaves, or added to stir-fried foods at the last moment; overcooking destroys the flavor of the leaves. The sprouted seedlings are good in salads.

Good with eggs, fish and seafood, mushrooms, poultry, rice, and as a garnish for most vegetables, especially sweet roots such as carrots and parsnips. **Combines well with** basil, chives, ginger, lemon balm, lemon grass, marjoram, sesame.

Fresh leaves

Mitsuba means "three leaves" in Japanese, from the three leaflets that make up the leaf. The meaning is echoed in the English name trefoil.

MARIGOLD
Calendula officinalis and Tagetes species

Marigolds are used in many different ways. The dried, ground petals of pot marigold (*C. officinalis*) and French marigold (*T. patula*) are prized in the Georgian republic; in Mexico and the southern US, Mexican mint marigold (*T. lucida*) is used as a tarragon substitute; in Peru, huacatay (*T. minuta*) is an essential flavoring; in Europe, fresh petals are used as a garnish and in salads.

Pot marigold *C. officinalis*
This marigold is a long-lived annual with pale green, lance-shaped leaves and single or double flowers. The petals and young leaves should be used immediately after picking.

DRIED PETALS
Dried pot marigold petals from the Republic of Georgia have a sweet, musky aroma with hints of citrus peel.

Culinary uses

Apart from adding a lively note to salads, marigold petals have long been used to color food and give it a slightly pungent flavor. Fresh petals can be added to cookies and small cakes, to custards, savory butters, and soups. Dried petals were often used to adulterate saffron; they can be used as an inexpensive substitute for coloring rice.

In the Republic of Georgia, dried marigold petals are an essential flavoring, used in spice mixtures and with other aromatic staples (chili peppers, garlic, walnuts). Georgians prefer the French marigold, and the flavor blends particularly well with cinnamon and cloves.

They call it Imeretian saffron after the province of Imereti, where the dried petals are highly appreciated.

Mint marigold leaves are used with other indigenous American foods – avocado, corn, squash, tomatoes – as well as with fish, chicken, and other foods that marry well with tarragon. They also combine well with melon, summer berries, and stone fruits.

Huacatay, also called black mint, is strongly aromatic with citrus and eucalypt notes and a bitter aftertaste. It is hard to find fresh outside South America, but is sold as a paste in jars in the US. Use with chili peppers to season grilled meats, soups, and stews.

Mexican mint marigold *T. lucida*

The long, narrow leaves of Mexican mint marigold smell more of anise than mint, with light notes of hay and some spicy warmth. The plant's other common names, winter or Mexican tarragon, refer to its tarragon-like taste.

French marigold *T. patula*

This marigold species is a bushy annual with divided, toothed leaves and flat single or frilly double flowers that vary in color from yellow to deep orange.

sweet herbs

BASIL

Ocimum species

Lightly brushing basil leaves releases an aroma that promises warmth and sunlight – in every Greek village the intoxicating fragrance of basil fills the air. Basil belongs to the mint family, as is clear from the minty, anise notes that accompany its sweetness. Native to tropical Asia, where it has been cultivated for 3,000 years, it is now grown almost everywhere where the climate is warm enough.

Sweet basil *O. basilicum*

Also called Genoese basil, this plant has large, bright green, silky leaves and small, white flowers. Good for all Western cooking, it is the best basil for pesto, pistou, and tomato salads. It combines very well with garlic. One way to preserve the leaves is to put them in a jar with an airtight lid, layer lightly with salt, and cover with olive oil. Kept in the refrigerator, the leaves eventually blacken, but they flavor the oil beautifully.

TASTING NOTES

Sweet basil has a complex sweet, spicy aroma with notes of clove and anise. The flavor is warm, peppery, and clove-like with underlying mint and anise tones. Purple (opal) basil, bush basil, lettuce basil, and 'Ruffles' basils have rather similar flavors (*pp.23–24*).

PARTS USED

Fresh leaves; add buds from flowerspikes to salads or use as a garnish.

BUYING AND STORING

Most basil leaves bruise and wilt easily, so avoid bunches with drooping or blackened leaves. Store for 2–3 days in damp paper towel or a plastic bag in the refrigerator vegetable crisper. Thai basil (*p.25*) is more sturdy and will keep for 5–6 days. Basil leaves will freeze well for up to 3 months; one of the best ways is to purée them with a little water or olive oil and freeze in ice-cube trays.

GROW YOUR OWN

Most basils are tender annuals. Basil grows easily from seed, and needs a sheltered, sunny position in rich, well-drained soil. In cooler climates it prefers a greenhouse or a windowsill. Delay flowering and encourage bushiness by pinching out the tops. Harvest until the first frost.

Culinary uses

In Western cooking, basil is the natural companion of tomatoes, whether in salad, sauce, or soup. It is a good flavoring for poultry too – combine softened butter with chopped basil, garlic, grated lemon rind, and a few bread crumbs, then work the mixture under the skin of a chicken or chicken pieces before baking or pot-roasting. Use basil with fish and seafood, especially lobster and scallops, and with roast veal and lamb. It also has an affinity with raspberries. Purple basil makes a pretty, pale pink vinegar.

Sweet basil turns black when cooked in a tomato sauce or other acid medium, but retains its flavor. It quickly loses its aroma when cooked, so use it in a dish for depth of flavor, then stir in a little more to add fragrance when the cooking is finished. Basil leaves can be torn, or chopped or shredded with a knife, but cutting bruises them and they darken quickly.

Essential to pesto and pistou.
Good with corn, cream cheese, eggplant, eggs, lemon, mozzarella cheese, olives, pasta, peas, pizza, potatoes, rice, tomatoes, white beans, zucchini.
Combines well with capers, chives, cilantro, garlic, marjoram, oregano, mint, parsley, rosemary, thyme.

Purple basil *O.b.* var. *purpurascens*

This handsome plant, also called opal basil, has purple or almost black leaves and pink flowers. It is highly aromatic, with clear notes of mint and clove. Use with rice and grains and to add a splash of color to salads.

Other basils

These basils tend to have names that indicate their aroma or appearance. All have the underlying sweet, warm, clove-anise aroma of sweet basil, but different aspects are dominant: pepper, cinnamon, lemon.

Bush basil *O. b.* var. *minimum*

Also called Greek basil, this makes a compact bush with small leaves, white flowers, and a peppery aroma. It is easy to grow in a pot. Use as sweet basil.

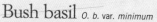

O. b. 'Cinnamon'

Native to Mexico, this variety has a sweet scent with clear cinnamon notes. Serve it with bean and legume dishes and with spicy, stir-fried vegetables.

Lettuce basil *O. b.* var. *crispum*

It is excellent in salads, or chopped and mixed with diced tomato and extra virgin olive oil to make a pasta dressing. Lettuce basil is much prized in southern Italy.

Asian basils

Asian basils are as numerous as Western basils. Their flavors differ from those of Western basils because of the different chemical constituents of the essential oils. The dominant aroma constituent of sweet basil (*p.22*) is linalool (floral) with some methyl chavicol (anise) and a little eugenol (clove), but in Asian basils methyl chavicol is dominant with some eugenol and a little camphor.

Thai basil *O. b. horapa*

Thai bai horapa has a heady, sweet, peppery aroma and a warm, lingering, anise-licorice flavor.

Lemon basil *O. b. citriodorum*

This bushy, compact basil has a clean, lemon fragrance. In Indonesia, where it is called kemangie, it is fried with fish and seafood. Add it to salads, and scatter over poached scallops or grilled fish.

Holy basil *O. sanctum*

Holy basil, or bai gaprow, is intensely aromatic with a spicy, sweet pungency, hints of mint and camphor, and a touch of muskiness. If you can't find it, use sweet basil and a few mint leaves. The flavor is enhanced by cooking; when raw, the taste is slightly bitter. It is the essential ingredient in a Thai dish of stir-fried chicken with chili peppers and basil, and is much used in meat curries.

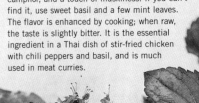

Culinary uses

Basil flavors Southeast-Asian salads, stir-fried dishes, soups, and curries. It is added at the end of cooking so that the aromatic leaves balance the spices in the dish. It is also used in Thai green curry paste.

Good with beef, chicken, coconut milk, fish and seafood, noodles, pork, rice.

Combines well with chili, cilantro leaf and root, galangal, garlic, ginger, kaffir lime, krachai, lemon grass, tamarind, turmeric.

BAY
Laurus nobilis

The bay tree is native to the eastern Mediterranean, but has long been cultivated in northern Europe and the Americas. It came to symbolize wisdom and glory to the Greeks and Romans, who crowned kings, poets, Olympic champions, and victorious generals with wreaths of its glossy, leathery leaves. Although there are several varieties of bay, only *L. nobilis* is used in the kitchen.

TASTING NOTES

Bay has a sweet, balsamic aroma with notes of nutmeg and camphor, and a cooling astringency. Fresh leaves are slightly bitter, but the bitterness fades if you keep them for a day or two. Fully dried leaves have a potent flavor and are best when dried only recently.

PARTS USED

Fresh and dried leaves.

BUYING AND STORING

Fresh leaves can be used from a tree, but are less bitter if kept until wilted. To dry completely, lay leaves flat in a dark, well-aired place and leave until brittle. If stored in an airtight container, dried leaves will keep their aroma and flavor for at least a year; stale leaves have no flavor.

GROW YOUR OWN

Although bay does best in warm regions, it will survive in a sheltered, sunny position in cooler climates. It is a good container plant, and growing it like this has the advantage that it can be moved indoors for the winter where not hardy. In warm climates it produces small, yellow flowers in spring, followed by purple berries (which are not edible). Leaves can be picked throughout the year.

Fresh leaves
Fresh leaves need to be crushed or rubbed to release their aromatic compounds. Bay is indispensable in French and Mediterranean cooking.

Bouquet garni
A bouquet garni is a bundle of herbs used to flavor slow-cooked dishes. The classic includes a few sprigs of thyme and parsley with a bay leaf.

DRIED LEAVES
Dried bay leaves should remain a mat, sage green, and not turn yellow or brown. Crumble or grind the leaves only when you need them.

Culinary uses

Bay leaves yield their flavor slowly, so they are useful in stocks, soups, stews, sauces, marinades, and pickles. Put a leaf or two on top of a homemade pâté or terrine before baking it; add bay to any fish stew, or combine with lemon and fennel when filling the cavity of a fish to be baked; thread leaves onto kebabs (soak dried leaves in water first), or add them to a pilaf. Bay is always included in a bouquet garni, and to flavor the milk for béchamel sauce. It goes well with beans, lentils, and tomatoes, especially to flavor a tomato sauce.

The Turks use bay in steamed and slow-cooked lamb dishes, the Moroccans in chicken and lamb tagines; the French partner it with beef in Provençal daubes. Bay also gives a pleasant, unusual, spicy fragrance to baked custards and rice pudding and to poached fruit dishes. In Turkish spice bazaars, boxes of dried figs are often lined with bay leaves.

Two or three bay leaves flavor a dish for four to six people; if you put in too many, the flavor will be too strong. Remove the leaves before serving. Note also that in India, parts of the Caribbean, and South America, leaves of other species may be called bay leaves.

Essential to bouquets garnis, béchamel sauce.

Good with beef, chestnuts, chicken, citrus fruits, fish, game, lamb, lentils, rice, tomatoes, white beans.

Combines well with allspice, garlic, juniper, marjoram, oregano, parsley, sage, savory, thyme.

SWEET CICELY

Myrrhis odorata

Sweet cicely is an underrated herb, a natural sweetener with a fine flavor, and its leaves remain green and edible from early spring to late autumn. A perennial indigenous to upland pastures from the far west of Europe to the Caucasus, it is long naturalized in northern Europe and is now cultivated in other temperate zones.

TASTING NOTES

Sweet cicely has an attractive, musky aroma with notes of lovage and anise; the flavor tends more to anise with a hint of celery and a pleasing sweetness. The whole plant is aromatic. The unripe seeds have the strongest flavor and a nutty texture. The glossy, black, ripe seeds have less flavor and are fibrous and chewy.

PARTS USED

Fresh leaves, flowers, and green seeds. In the past raw roots were added to salads or boiled and eaten as a vegetable.

BUYING AND STORING

Plants are available from herb nurseries, and can also be grown from seed. Sweet cicely is not available from supermarkets. The leaves are best used soon after picking, but they will keep for 2–3 days in damp paper towel or a plastic bag in the vegetable crisper of the refrigerator.

GROW YOUR OWN

Sweet cicely is easy to grow and prefers rich, moist soil and semi-shade. It self-seeds readily. Cut back the whole plant after flowering to encourage new growth. Cut leaves between spring and autumn. Harvest the flowers in spring, and the green, unripe seeds in summer.

Culinary uses

The leaves and green seeds reduce the tartness of fruits such as gooseberries and rhubarb when cooked together, although the flavor of the herb itself is dissipated. Leaves and seeds add an anise note to fruit salads and cream-cheese desserts, and sweetness and a hint of spice to cakes, breads, and fruit pies. Sweet cicely is a useful herb for savory dishes too, but to retain the flavor it is best to add it at the end of the cooking time. Young leaf tips give a subtle flavor to green salads and cucumber, and to cream and yogurt sauces made to accompany fish or seafood. Chop leaves into omelettes and clear soups, and stir them into a purée of carrot, parsnip, or pumpkin to enhance the sweetness. Use leaves as a garnish for cheese, and flowers to decorate salads. **Good with** apricots, gooseberries, nectarines, peaches, rhubarb, strawberries, root vegetables; chicken, scallops, shrimp. **Combines well with** chervil, chives, lemon balm, lemon verbena, mint, vanilla.

Fresh sprigs

By late spring the large, feathery plant bears sweetly scented, lacy, white flowers, followed by large, attractive seedheads.

PANDAN
Pandanus amaryllifolius, P. tectorius

TASTING NOTES

Pandan leaf smells sweetly fresh and floral, lightly musky, with notes of new-mown grass. The taste is pleasantly grassy and floral. Leaves have to be bruised or cooked to release their flavor. Kewra essence has a sweet, delicate musk and rose aroma.

PARTS USED

Leaves, flowers.

BUYING AND STORING

Fresh pandan leaves may be found in Asian markets. They keep well in a plastic bag in the refrigerator for 2–3 weeks. Neither frozen nor dried pandan can match fresh leaves for fragrance. Bottled leaf extract has an unnaturally bright color and quickly loses what aroma it has. Pandan powder has a light grassiness that fades after a few months. Kewra essence or kewra water (essence mixed with water) will keep for 2–3 years if tightly closed and stored away from strong light.

HARVESTING

Pandan trees, with their shiny, sword-like leaves growing spirally around the trunk, can be seen in gardens throughout southern Asia. They grow easily, especially in damp areas. Leaves are harvested at any time; flowers are at their best soon after they open.

Pandan or screwpine species grow in the tropics from India to Southeast Asia, northern Australia, and the Pacific islands. The leaves of *P. amaryllifolius* are used as a flavoring and a wrapping for food. Kewra essence, a favorite flavoring of the Moghul emperors of India, is extracted from *P. tectorius* flowers.

Culinary uses

To use pandan leaves, pound or scrape them with the prongs of a fork to release their flavor, then tie in a loose knot so that the fibers do not come loose.

Add a leaf or two to rice before cooking to give it a light fragrance, as they do in Malaysia and Singapore. Cooks there also use pandan leaf as a flavoring for pancakes, cakes, and creamy desserts made with sticky rice or tapioca. A knotted leaf is sometimes added to a soup or curry, and in Sri Lanka it adds its flavor to curry powder. Leaves are also used to wrap food. Thai cooks steam or fry parcels of pandan-wrapped chicken or weave leaves as containers for desserts.

Kewra essence is used in India to flavor pilafs and meat dishes as well as sweets and kulfi. It can be diluted with a little water and sprinkled into a dish just before serving. It also gives a special flavor to homemade lemonade.

Good with chicken, coconut, curried dishes, palm sugar, rice.

Combines well with chili, cilantro, galangal, ginger, kaffir lime, lemon grass.

Fresh leaves

Juice from the leaves is used for coloring food; to extract the juice, put 4–5 coarsely chopped leaves into a blender with a little water.

LAVENDER
Lavandula species

TASTING NOTES

Lavender has a penetrating, sweetly floral, and spicy aroma with lemon and mint notes; the taste echoes the aroma with undertones of camphor and a touch of bitterness in the aftertaste. The flowers have the strongest fragrance, but leaves can also be used.

PARTS USED

Fresh and dried flowers; leaves.

BUYING AND STORING

Well-stocked garden centers and herb nurseries have plentiful supplies of a variety of lavenders from spring to autumn. Fresh lavender flowers and leaves will keep in a plastic bag in the refrigerator for up to a week. Dried lavender will keep for a year or more. To dry flowers, hang stems in small bunches or spread on trays; when fully dry, rub the flowers from the stems and store in an airtight container.

GROW YOUR OWN

Lavender needs an open, sunny position and well-drained soil, whether in the garden or a container. The flowers are best harvested just before they are fully open, when their essential oils are most potent. Harvest leaves at any time during the growing season.

The sight of the deep purple-blue lavender fields shimmering in the heat as you travel down the Rhône valley in France is, for me, the first real indication of reaching the warm south. Native to the Mediterranean region, lavender became a popular garden plant in Tudor England. Today, lavender is grown in many parts of the world for display, for the kitchen, and for its aromatic oils.

English lavender
L. angustifolia

The gray-green foliage and lilac, purple, or white flowers of this evergreen shrub make it one of the most attractive garden plants. Also called common lavender, it is the best lavender for the cook because of its lower camphor content.

FRESH LEAVES
Like rosemary, lavender has tough leaves that must be chopped finely; flowers also have a firm base, but petals can be plucked out.

DRIED FLOWERS
Soft, floral-scented, English lavender is no less prized for its oils than the intensely aromatic original lavender from the Mediterranean.

French lavender *L. stoechas*

Also called Spanish lavender, this bushy shrub has narrow, green leaves and purple flowers topped by purple bracts. Some varieties are hardy, others are half-hardy and may survive the winter in a sheltered spot. *L. stoechas* has a more pungent camphor note than *L. angustifolia*.

Culinary uses

Lavender is very potent and must be used sparingly. A few dried lavender flowers immersed in a jar of sugar for a week or so will give it a fine, sweet aroma. Alternatively, grind fresh lavender flowers and sugar to a powder – this gives a stronger flavor since grinding breaks down the buds and the sugar absorbs the aromatic oils. Use the sugar for baking and in desserts.

Fresh flowers can be chopped and added to a cake batter or sweet pastry or shortbread dough before baking. Scatter petals over a cake or dessert to decorate it. Add flowers to preserves toward the end of the cooking time, or to fruit compotes for a sweetly spiced note. Infuse flowers in cream, milk, syrup, or wine to flavor sorbets and other desserts. Lavender ice cream is very good, or try adding lavender to chocolate ice cream or mousse.

Lavender is successful in savory dishes, too. Chop leaves for a salad or scatter flowers over the top. Fold chopped flowers into cooked rice. Use chopped flowers and leaves to flavor a leg of lamb, or roast or casseroled rabbit, chicken, or pheasant. Add lavender to marinades and rubs. Lavender also makes an excellent vinegar.

Around the Mediterranean, lavender is used in herb mixtures. In Provence, France, it is blended with thyme, savory, and rosemary; in Morocco, it is sometimes used in ras el hanout.

Good with blackberries, blueberries, cherries, mulberries, plums, rhubarb, strawberries; and chicken, lamb, pheasant, rabbit.

Combines well with marjoram, oregano, parsley, perilla, rosemary, savory, thyme.

BEE BALM
Monarda didyma

Native to North America, the genus *Monarda* is named for the 16th-century Spanish physician, Nicolas Monardes, whose *Joyfull Newes Out of the Newe Founde Worlde* was the first American herbal. It is commonly called bee balm because the flowers attract bees. Another name, bergamot, probably derives from the similarity of the plant's aroma to that of the bergamot orange.

Culinary uses

Use only fresh, young leaves and flowers for cooking. Add shredded leaves and petals to green and fruit salads. Bee balm goes well with duck, chicken, and pork; it can be chopped into yogurt or cream for a sauce, or added to a salsa. Flowers are good in sandwiches with cream cheese and cucumber.

Good with apples, chicken, citrus fruits, duck, kiwi fruit, melon, papaya, pork, strawberries, tomatoes.

Combines well with chives, cresses, dill, fennel, garlic, lemon balm, mint, parsley, rosemary, thyme.

Other monardas

Wild bee balm, *M. fistulosa*, also known as horsemint, is less handsome and has a stronger and coarser fragrance than cultivated varieties. Use sparingly.

Another variety, *M. f.* var. *menthifolia*, resembles oregano in aroma and flavor and is sometimes used as a substitute for oregano in the southwestern US.

Fresh leaves
All the cultivated varieties of bee balm, with their showy whorls of different colored flowers and slightly different scents, can be used in the same way.

LEMON BALM
Melissa officinalis

Lemon balm is a perennial of the mint family, native to southern Europe and western Asia, and now cultivated widely in all temperate regions. With its crinkled, serrated leaves and tiny white or yellowish flowers, it is not a showy plant, but earns its place in the garden by attracting bees and by its agreeable lemon scent.

Culinary uses

Lemon balm's principal use is in a soothing, calming tea, made from fresh or dried leaves. Fresh leaves can be infused in summer punches or blended in smoothies. For cooking, the lemon-mint flavor of fresh leaves complements fish and poultry in sauces, stuffings, and marinades. Tear young leaves for green or tomato salads, or chop them to scatter over steamed or sautéed vegetables or to stir into rice or cracked wheat. Lemon balm makes a delicate herb butter and fragrant vinegar. The fresh flavor is good in fruit desserts and in creams and cakes. A strong tea, well sweetened, makes the basis for a good sorbet.

Good with apples, apricots, carrots, soft white cheeses, chicken, eggs, figs, fish, melon, mushrooms, nectarines, peaches, peas, summer berries, tomatoes, zucchini.

Combines well with bee balm, chervil, chives, dill, fennel, ginger, mint, nasturtium, parsley, sweet cicely.

TASTING NOTES

When crushed, the young leaves have a fresh, lingering, lemon scent and a mild lemon-mint flavor. The aroma is subtle and pleasant, and not as penetrating as that of lemon verbena or lemon grass. Large, older leaves have a musty flavor.

PARTS USED

Leaves, fresh and dried.

BUYING AND STORING

Seeds and plants may be bought from specialist nurseries. Fresh leaves will keep for 3–4 days in a plastic bag in the vegetable crisper in the refrigerator. To dry leaves, hang small bunches of stems in a dark, airy place. Crumble the leaves when completely dry and store in an airtight container. They should keep their flavor for 5–6 months.

GROW YOUR OWN

Lemon balm is easy to grow from seed or by dividing the root stock in spring or autumn. Plants should be cut back after flowering to encourage new growth. Balm grows vigorously and will spread readily unless kept in check: in a small garden it is best grown in a pot. Leaves should be harvested early in the season since they can become rank later on.

Fresh leaves
Always cook with fresh leaves, and use generous amounts because the aroma is delicate. The variegated form, *M. o.* 'Aurea', can also be used.

LEMON VERBENA

Aloysia citriodora

Lemon verbena is native to Chile and Argentina, and was taken to Europe by the Spaniards and to North America by a New England sea captain in the 18th century. In France, it was used by toilet-water manufacturers for its aromatic oils. Until 100 years ago it was widely grown as an ornamental garden plant; it certainly merits a place in any scented garden for its intoxicating, pure lemon fragrance.

TASTING NOTES

Lemon verbena has an intense, fresh lemon aroma. The taste echoes the aroma but is less strong; it is more lemony than a lemon, but lacks the tartness. Leaves keep their fragrance quite well when cooked. The aroma of dried leaves is retained for up to a year.

PARTS USED

Leaves, fresh and dried.

BUYING AND STORING

Specialist herb nurseries stock plants. Cut leaves can be kept for a day or two in the refrigerator. Sprigs can also be put in a glass of water for 24 hours. Leaves can be chopped and frozen in small pots or in ice cubes. To dry, hang stems in a dark, well-ventilated place. Dried lemon verbena is sold as a tisane, and that is the best use for dried leaves.

GROW YOUR OWN

Lemon verbena needs sun and well-drained soil. Leaves can be harvested throughout the growing season. Regular trimming will make the plant bushier, and it should be cut back in autumn to remove weak branches. It does not tolerate frost, so is best grown in a container and taken indoors in winter, when it will shed its leaves. Take outside only when frosts are over.

Culinary uses

Lemon verbena is a natural companion to fish and poultry: put some sprigs into the cavity, or chop and use in a stuffing or marinade. The vibrant, clean taste is also good with fatty meats such as pork and duck, in vegetable soup, and in a rice pilaf. Lemon verbena is used as a flavoring for desserts and drinks. Add sprigs to a syrup for poaching fruit, chop finely for a fruit salad or tart, or infuse in cream to make a fresh-scented ice cream. Lining a cake pan with leaves will give a lemon scent to a plain cake.

Good with apricots, carrots, chicken, fish, mushrooms, rice, zucchini.
Combines well with basil, chili, chives, cilantro, lemon thyme, mint, garlic.

Fresh sprigs
Add sprigs to iced tea or summer coolers, or make an infusion of fresh leaves. Lemon verbena makes one of the best and most refreshing of all teas.

SASSAFRAS
Sassafras albidum

Sassafras is an aromatic, ornamental tree native to the eastern US, from Maine to Florida. Native Americans showed early settlers how to make tea from the bark, roots, and leaves. The French-speaking Canadians (Cajuns) who went to Louisiana adopted a Choctaw method of using dried, ground sassafras leaves to flavor and thicken stews. The roots used to be an essential ingredient of root beer.

Culinary uses

Filé powder, or gumbo filé, made from dried, ground sassafras leaves, is only used in the cooking of Louisiana, but it is the key to the texture and flavor of many Cajun and Creole soups and stews. In particular, it is used in gumbo, a substantial, spicy soup made with a variety of vegetables, seafood, or meat and served with rice. The mucilaginous quality of filé helps thicken the dish, provided it is stirred in when the pan is removed from the heat; prolonged cooking makes filé tough and stringy. Some brands of filé powder contain other ground herbs, such as bay, oregano, sage, or thyme, in addition to ground sassafras leaf.

Dried leaves
The large leaves, which provide dramatic autumn colors, may have one, two, or three lobes, even on the same branch.

FILE POWDER
Filé powder is essential to create the rich texture of Louisiana dishes. It also serves as a condiment to accompany them.

SORREL

Rumex acetosa, R. scutatus

A member of the dock family, sorrel grows wild in meadowlands throughout much of Europe and western Asia, and it is well worth growing in the garden. Garden sorrel, *R. acetosa*, is the common variety; French or buckler leaf sorrel, *R. scutatus*, has a more delicate, lemony flavor.

Culinary uses

Sorrel is high in vitamins A and C, and also in oxalic acid, which gives the herb its sour taste. It is best served in combination with other foods. It makes a good soup with potato and a rich sauce for fish with butter, stock and cream.

Good with chicken, cucumber, eggs, fish (especially salmon), leeks, lentils, lettuce, mussels, pork, spinach, tomatoes, veal, watercress.
Combines well with borage, chervil, chives, dill, lovage, parsley, tarragon.

AGASTACHE
Agastache species

TASTING NOTES

Anise hyssop has a sweet, anise aroma and flavor; it has a natural sweetness, unlike many herbs that are bitter when tasted alone. Korean mint smells of eucalypt and mint, but the taste resembles that of anise hyssop, with a lingering anise aftertaste.

PARTS USED

Fresh leaves; flowers for garnishes.

BUYING AND STORING

Some specialist nurseries stock plants. Leaves are quite sturdy and will keep in a plastic bag in the vegetable crisper of the refrigerator for 4–5 days. Leaves can be frozen, but they are best used fresh. Dry leaves only to make teas – otherwise don't bother.

GROW YOUR OWN

Anise hyssop and Korean mint prefer a sheltered, well-drained spot in full sun. Both can be grown from seed. After 2–3 years plants can be divided and replanted. If you leave some flowers to seed, agastaches will self-seed, but the new plants come up quite late in the year. Harvest young leaves throughout the growing season. They are most aromatic just before the plant flowers.

The agastaches are handsome, perennials of the mint family that are just becoming known in Europe. Two are particularly worth the cook's attention – anise hyssop, *A. foeniculum*, native to North America, and Korean mint, *A. rugosa*, native to eastern Asia. Mexican giant hyssop, *A. mexicana*, is half-hardy and grows wild in Mexico, where the leaves and flowers are used to make a tea.

FLOWERS
Anise hyssop smells of anise and its flowers resemble those of hyssop, but it is not related to either plant.

Anise hyssop
A. foeniculum

Anise hyssop, also called licorice mint, is an upright, branched plant with gray-green, oval leaves tinged with purple. The showy, lilac flowerspikes appear in late summer and attract bees.

CHERVIL

Anthriscus cerefolium

Native to southern Russia, the Caucasus, and southeastern Europe, chervil was probably introduced to northern Europe by the Romans. A traditional symbol of new life, the arrival of chervil in markets signals springtime, when chervil sauces and soups appear on menus in France, Germany, and Holland. Often seen in restaurants as a garnish, chervil deserves to be more widely used in domestic cooking.

Fresh leaves

Chervil grows quickly and can be harvested 6–8 weeks after sowing, but its lifespan is short – once it flowers it is of no use in the kitchen. Be rigorous about cutting out flower stems and harvest frequently, cutting outer leaves first to encourage new growth at the center of the plant.

TASTING NOTES

Chervil is sweetly aromatic. The taste is subtle and soothing, with light anise notes and hints of parsley, caraway, and pepper.

PARTS USED

Fresh leaves; flowers for garnish.

BUYING AND STORING

Chervil is not an herb for long keeping: in a plastic bag or in damp paper towel, it will keep for 2–3 days in the vegetable crisper of the refrigerator. Chopped and frozen in small containers it will keep for 3–4 months. Chervil butter can also be frozen. Dried chervil has almost no flavor and is not worth buying.

GROW YOUR OWN

Chervil is easy to grow from seed, and prefers rich, moist soil in semi-shade. Sow seed where you want the plants to grow, because chervil doesn't like to be transplanted. It does best in cool temperatures, so in summer, plant it between taller plants that will provide shade. Old leaves turn pink or yellow and no longer have a fresh flavor. Sow the first batch of seeds toward the end of winter, and then sow every 3–4 weeks to ensure a continuing supply.

Culinary uses

Chervil is one of the indispensable herbs of French cooking: in classic fines herbes it is combined with chives, parsley, and tarragon. Fines herbes – or chervil alone – stirred into eggs will make an excellent omelette or scrambled egg dish. In Holland and Belgium, there is a long tradition of making chervil soup, either based on potato and shallot or a richer version that uses cream and egg yolks.

Chervil is delicious in consommés, and gives a delicate flavor to vinaigrettes and to butter or cream sauces to serve with fish, poultry, and vegetables. It is a great addition to salads: try it in a warm potato salad or a beet salad with shallots or chives. Chervil is sometimes used with tarragon in béarnaise sauce, and its flavor can usually be detected in Frankfurt green sauce. A small amount of chervil brings out the flavor of other herbs, but you can use it lavishly on its own – for example, scatter it generously over freshly cooked vegetables. If you are using it in a hot dish, stir it in when the cooking is at an end, because the aroma and flavor quickly dissipate with heat.

Curly chervil, *A. c. crispum*, has the same properties as the flat-leafed variety.
Essential to fines herbes.
Good with asparagus, beets, carrots, cream cheese, eggs, fava beans, fennel, fish and seafood, green beans, lettuce, mushrooms, peas, potatoes, poultry, tomatoes, veal.
Combines well with basil, chives, cresses, dill, hyssop, lemon thyme, mint, mustard, parsley, salad burnet, tarragon.

Fines herbes

This classic French flavoring for egg, fish, and poultry dishes is a combination of chervil, chives, parsley, and tarragon.

TARRAGON

Artemisia dracunculus

TASTING NOTES

The leaves are sweetly aromatic, with hints of pine, anise, or licorice; the flavor is strong yet subtle, with spicy anise and basil notes and a sweetish aftertaste. Long cooking diminishes the aroma but the flavor is not lost.

Native to Siberia and western Asia, tarragon was unknown in Europe until the Arabs introduced it when they ruled Spain. During the 16th and 17th centuries, the development of classic French cooking extended its use in the kitchen. Indeed, the best cultivated variety is usually called French tarragon (or, in Germany, German tarragon) to distinguish it from the inferior Russian variety.

PARTS USED

Fresh leaves and sprigs.

BUYING AND STORING

Supermarkets sell tarragon in small quantities, so it is better to grow your own. Avoid the Russian variety when buying plants. Young sprigs keep for 4–5 days in a plastic bag in the vegetable crisper of the refrigerator. To dry, hang stems in bundles in an airy, dark place. Dried they lose much of their aroma; freezing the leaves, whole or chopped, retains more of the flavor.

GROW YOUR OWN

French tarragon can be propagated by cuttings or in spring by division of the brittle, white rhizomes – do this every 3 years to preserve the flavor of the plant. The more vigorous Russian tarragon will grow from seed. Tarragon needs a rich, dry soil and much sun. Until well established the roots of French tarragon may need winter protection.

French tarragon *A. d.* var. *sativa*

This tarragon has mid-green leaves and is the preferred culinary variety. The leaves can be harvested when required, and whole stems removed for drying in midsummer.

Culinary uses

Tarragon is an essential ingredient in French cooking, with fish, poultry, and egg dishes. Used discreetly, it lends a pleasant, deep note to green salads. It is very good in marinades for meat and game, and for flavoring goat cheeses and feta preserved in olive oil. Whole stems can be used under fish or with roast chicken and rabbit – "tarragon chicken" appears in nearly every cook's repertoire.

Tarragon makes one of the most versatile of herb vinegars and is often used in mustards and butters.

It adds a fresh, herbal fragrance to mushrooms, artichokes, and ragouts of summer vegetables; with tomatoes it is almost as good as basil. Use tarragon in moderation and it will enhance the flavor of other herbs.

Essential to fines herbes and similar herb mixtures, to béarnaise, ravigote, and tartar sauces.

Good with artichokes, asparagus, eggs, fish and seafood, potatoes, poultry, salsify, tomatoes, zucchini.

Combines well with basil, bay, capers, chervil, chives, dill, parsley, salad herbs.

Other tarragons

Russian tarragon, *A. d.* var. *inodora,* or sometimes *A. dracunculoides,* is lighter in color and more coarse in appearance, and has a bitter taste. It is best avoided. When buying a tarragon plant, check that the label says French tarragon; if the type of tarragon is not specified, it may be the Russian variety.

Mexican tarragon, *Tagetes lucida,* is a species of marigold (*p.21*) that is often used in the southern states instead of French tarragon. It has a more pronounced licorice flavor.

Bouquet garni for fish

Intended to be added to the liquid of slow-cooked fish dishes, this bouquet garni comprises tarragon, thyme, parsley, and a strip of lemon peel.

DILL
Anethum graveolens

TASTING NOTES

Dill leaves have a clean, fragrant aroma of anise and lemon. The taste is of anise and parsley, mild but sustained. The seeds smell like a sweet caraway due to carvone in the essential oil; the taste is of anise with a touch of sharpness and a lingering warmth.

An annual plant native to southern Russia, western Asia, and the eastern Mediterranean, dill is widely grown for its feathery leaves (often called dill weed) and its seed. Indian dill, *A. g.* subsp. *sowa*, is grown primarily for its seed, which is lighter in color, longer, and narrower than European dill seed and has a more pungent taste. It is preferred for curry mixtures.

PARTS USED

Fresh and dried leaves; seeds.

BUYING AND STORING

Choose a bunch that looks crisp and fresh. If you have a large quantity, use it quickly; after 2–3 days kept in a plastic bag in the refrigerator it will droop. Dried dill stored in an airtight container will keep its flavor for up to a year. Similarly stored seed has a shelf life of 2 years. Ground dill seed does not keep.

GROW YOUR OWN

Dill is easy to grow from seed. Sow in a sheltered, sunny spot with well-drained soil in spring, and water well. Successive sowings will provide plants throughout the season. Dill seedlings are frail, so make sure the ground is weed-free. Flowerheads left to ripen will readily self-seed. Do not transplant; the long tap root is easily damaged. Avoid planting dill and fennel close to each other or they will cross-pollinate and create hybrids.

Fresh leaves

Freezing preserves the flavor of dill better than drying. Freeze the stems whole in a plastic bag and cut off sprigs when needed. Add dill leaves at the end of cooking because they lose their flavor if overheated.

FRONDS
The feathery fronds of *A. graveolens* resemble fennel, although the dill plant is much smaller.

DRYING LEAVES

Dill leaves can be dried, either by spreading them on a cloth and leaving in a dark, warm, well-ventilated place for a few days, or in the microwave. Dried leaves retain some of the aroma and flavor of the fresh plant.

SEEDS

The seeds are oval and flattish with five ribs, two of which form a broader rim. They are extremely light: 10,000 weigh less than 1oz (25g). Harvest seeds when they are light brown and fully formed; put the seedheads in a large paper bag and leave in a warm place until dry. When they have dried, rub the seedheads between your hands to separate seeds from husks. Use the seeds for slow-cooked foods.

Culinary uses

Fresh dill is an excellent partner for fish and seafood. Scandinavian dishes include herrings marinated with dill, gravad lax (salmon cured with salt and dill and served with a mustard and dill sauce), and crab, scallops, or shrimp with a creamy dill sauce.

In northern and central Europe, dill is used with root vegetables, cabbage, cauliflower, and cucumber. Some Russian cooks use it in borscht, their classic beet soup, and dill combined with sour cream or yogurt and a little mustard also makes a good sauce for beets. German cooks make a similar sauce, but replace the mustard with horseradish and serve it with braised beef. In Greece, dill is added to stuffed grape leaves. In Turkey and Iran, dill flavors rice, fava beans, zucchini, and celery root. Spinach with dill and shallots is a standard Iranian dish, echoed in a lentil and spinach dish of northern India that uses both dill leaves and seeds. Don't forget dill for salads and salad dressings, especially for potato salad.

Both leaves and seeds are used in pickling, as in the crunchy dill-pickled cucumbers of a New York deli and the garlicky version popular in Poland, Russia, and Iran. Seeds are added to breads and cakes in Scandinavia, where they are also used to flavor vinegar. In India, seeds and leaves are used in curry powders and masalas.

Leaves good with beets, carrots, celery root, cucumber, eggs, fava beans, fish and seafood, potatoes, rice, spinach, zucchini.

Leaves combine well with basil, capers, garlic, horseradish, mustard, paprika, parsley.

Seeds good with cabbage, onion, potatoes, pumpkin, vinegar.

Seeds combine well with chili, coriander seed, cumin, garlic, ginger, mustard seed, turmeric.

FENNEL

Foeniculum vulgare

This tall, hardy, graceful perennial, indigenous to the Mediterranean and now naturalized in many parts of the world, is one of the oldest cultivated plants. The Romans enjoyed fennel shoots as a vegetable; the Chinese and Indians valued fennel as a condiment and digestive aid. Today in India, fennel water is used to treat colic in babies. The herb should not be confused with the bulbous sweet or Florence fennel, *F. v.* var. *dulce*, which is eaten as a vegetable.

Green fennel *F. vulgare*

Green fennel is a tall, stately plant with tangled, feathery foliage. All parts of the fennel plant are edible; the roots are no longer eaten, but the leaves, stems, and fruits (seed) are esteemed as flavorings. Fennel's anise character derives from anethole, the main constituent of its essential oil, which is most concentrated in the seed.

STEMS
Stems have a mild flavor that is retained when they are dried.

Culinary uses

In spring, fennel gives a fresh, lively note to salads and sauces. Later in the season a garnish of flowers or a sprinkling of pollen gives an anise fragrance to cold soups, chowders, and grilled fish.

Fennel is an excellent foil for oily fish. The Sicilians use it liberally in their pasta with sardines. In Provence, France, whole fish such as red mullet are baked or grilled on a bed of fresh or dried fennel stems, which imparts a delicate flavor.

Pollen gives a more heady flavor to fish, seafood, grilled vegetables, pork chops, and Italian breads.

Fennel seed can be added to pickles, soups, and breads – try combining ground fennel and nigella to flavor bread, as is done in Iraq. In Greece, leaves or seeds are combined with feta cheese and olives to make a well-flavored bread. Fennel seeds flavor sauerkraut in Alsace and Germany, and Italians use them with roast pork and in finocchiona, the renowned salami of Florence.

Fennel seed is one of the constituents of five spice powder, the principal Chinese spice blend used mostly with meat and poultry. Bengal, in northeast India, also has a five spice mixture, panch phoron, with fennel as an ingredient; the mixture is used with vegetables, beans, and lentils. Elsewhere in the Indian subcontinent, fennel appears in garam masala, in spiced gravies for vegetables or lamb, and in some sweet dishes. Indians also chew fennel seed after a meal as a breath-freshener and digestive aid.

Good with beans, beets, cabbage, cucumber, duck, fish and seafood, leeks, lentils, pork, potatoes, rice, tomatoes.

Combines well with chervil, cinnamon, cumin, fenugreek, lemon balm, mint, nigella, parsley, Sichuan pepper, thyme.

Bronze fennel *F. v.* 'Purpureum'

This is a less vigorous plant than green fennel and has a milder aroma and flavor.

LEAVES
Only young fennel leaves are suitable for use in the kitchen. They have a mild taste and are best used soon after picking.

SEEDS
Fennel seed has a stronger flavor than the leaves and a bittersweet aftertaste. Dry-roasting the seed brings out the sweetness. Seed color varies from light brown to greenish-yellow – the latter is the best quality. It is best to keep seed and grind it as needed.

MINT
Mentha species

One of the most popular flavors in the world, mint is at once cooling and warming, with a sweet fragrance. Native to southern Europe and the Mediterranean, mints have long naturalized throughout the temperate world. They hybridize easily, leading to some confusion in their naming, but for the cook they broadly divide into two groups: spearmint and peppermint.

TASTING NOTES

Spearmint is mellow and refreshing, with a sweet-sharp, pleasantly pungent flavor backed by hints of lemon. Peppermint has pronounced menthol notes and a fiery bite, yet is also slightly sweet, tangy, and spicy with a fresh, cool aftertaste.

PARTS USED

Leaves, fresh and dried; flowers for salads and garnishes.

BUYING AND STORING

Bunches of fresh spearmint will keep for 2 days in a glass of water in the kitchen, or in the refrigerator. Leaves can be chopped and frozen in small containers or mixed with a little water or oil and frozen in ice-cube trays. Mint dries well; pick before flowering and hang bunches in a dry, airy place, or dry sprigs in a low oven or microwave. Store dried mint in an airtight container.

GROW YOUR OWN

Mints are perennial plants and are easy to grow. They prefer partial shade or full sun, and need lots of water. They have a spreading habit, so unless you have space for mint to run wild it is best to grow it in a pot. Otherwise, plant in a large, bottomless pot or bucket.

Fresh leaves
The most widely grown mint, spearmint or garden mint (*M. spicata*), has pointed leaves and bears lilac flowers in late summer. This mint and its cultivated varieties suit all recipes calling for mint. Leaves can be picked thoughout the growing season, but are best harvested shortly before flowering, when the essential oils are at their strongest. The aroma of mints is due to menthol, which also leaves cooling and mild numbing sensations in the mouth.

Culinary uses

Mint has many uses worldwide. Fresh and dried mints are not usually used interchangeably in recipes.

Fresh mint

Western cooks use mint to flavor carrots, eggplant, peas, potatoes, tomatoes, and zucchini. Mint goes well with chicken, pork, veal, and the traditional spring lamb, whether as a marinade, mint jelly, mint sauce, or a salsa. Sauce paloise (a béarnaise sauce made with mint instead of tarragon) is a good accompaniment to grilled fish and chicken.

In the Middle East, mint is essential to tabbouleh and is part of the bowl of fresh herbs and salad vegetables that accompanies mezze. In Vietnam, it is added to salads and to platters of herbs that accompany spring rolls. Mint also finds its way into Southeast-Asian dipping sauces, sambals, and curries. The cooling notes of mint make it the perfect herb for chilled Iranian yogurt and cucumber soup, and the Indians emphasize its refreshing qualities in chutneys and raitas. Indian cooks also use the freshness of mint to counter the warmth of spices in vegetable and meat dishes. In much of South America, mint is combined with chili peppers, parsley, and oregano as a flavoring for slow-cooked dishes; Mexicans use a little with meatballs and chicken.

Mint's refreshing effect enhances fruit salads, fruit punches, and, of course, a mint julep. It makes a surprisingly good iced parfait, and minty notes are a welcome addition to several kinds of chocolate desserts and cakes. **Combines well with** basil, cardamom, cloves, cumin, dill, fenugreek, ginger, marjoram, oregano, paprika, parsley, pepper, sumac, thyme.

Dried mint

Around the eastern Mediterranean and in the Arab countries, dried mint is often preferred to fresh. In Greece, dried mint, sometimes with oregano and cinnamon, seasons keftedes (meatballs) and the filling for grape leaves; the Cypriots use it for their Easter cheesecakes, called flaounes. Cacik, the Turkish cucumber and yogurt salad, is best with dried mint. A teaspoon of dried mint, quickly fried in a little olive oil or clarified butter and added just before serving, imparts a fine, lively aroma to some Turkish and Iranian dishes. Try it with lentil and bean soups, and lamb or vegetable stews.

DRIED LEAVES
Spearmint is the dried mint most commonly found commercially. The aroma is pungent and concentrated but lacks the sweetness of fresh.

TASTING NOTES

Raw, dried garlic is pungent and hot; green garlic is milder. The disulphate allicin is formed when raw garlic is cut, and this accounts for the smell that raw garlic leaves on the breath. Cooking garlic degrades the allicin, but forms other disulphates that have less odor.

PARTS USED

Bulbs.

BUYING AND STORING

Garlic is available all year round. Choose unbruised, firm heads without signs of mold or sprouting. If your garlic is sprouting, remove the indigestible green shoots. Store garlic in a cool, dry place. Dehydrated garlic flakes, granules, and powder are available, as are garlic paste, extract and juice. Smoked garlic is chic but not especially useful.

GROW YOUR OWN

Garlic is propagated by the cloves. It grows best in rich, moist soil in a sunny position. Perennial or biennial, it is extremely hardy and survives long periods of cold. Harvest when the tops dry out and begin to collapse. Pull up the whole plant and hang in the shade to dry. As harvested garlic dries, the skin becomes papery and the flavor intensifies.

GARLIC
Allium sativum

Garlic is native to the steppes of central Asia and spread first to the Middle East. It was one of the earliest cultivated herbs, but its early use was mainly medical and magical – except in ancient Egypt where it was eaten in quantity. When the first English settlers took it to America, it was still regarded as a medicinal herb. Today it is recognized for lowering blood pressure and cholesterol, but its culinary use has become vastly more important.

Fresh heads
At the beginning of the growing season, heads of new green garlic are succulent and mild, and have a soft, thick, white skin.

Culinary uses

If crushed with the flat blade of a heavy knife, dried garlic cloves are easy to peel. Once peeled, garlic can be pounded in a mortar. Avoid garlic presses because they can make the taste unpleasantly acrid.

Garlic can be used to enhance the flavor of many foods. Whole cloves cooked slowly have a mellow, nutty taste; cut garlic is more pungent, even when cooked. Similarly, a whole clove gently sautéed in oil and then removed will leave a delicate flavor: a minced clove leaves a much stronger one. Never let garlic burn or it will develop a bitter, acrid taste. Garlic roasted whole can accompany new potatoes or root vegetables. In European cooking, garlic is roasted with chicken or lamb; braised in wine; puréed, blanched, or sautéed. Young, green garlic can be used in summer vegetable stews without peeling. In Spain, young garlic shoots are fried for tapas. Raw garlic flavors salads, is rubbed over bread with tomato and oil, and is pounded with egg yolks and oil to make aïoli or, with nuts and basil, pesto. In Asia, where the consumption of garlic far exceeds that of the Mediterranean countries, its companions are lemon grass, fresh ginger, cilantro, chili peppers, and soy sauce. Garlic is used in stir-fried dishes, curry pastes, sambals, and nam prik. In Cuba, it is combined with cumin and citrus juice to make the ubiquitous table sauces called mojos. Garlic can also be steeped in oil for a few days, and in vinegar for at least two weeks. In Korea and Russia, garlic makes a much-loved pickle.

Essential to many sauces (aïoli, allioli, skordalia, rouille, tarator, pesto).

Good with almost anything savory.

Combines well with most herbs and spices.

DRIED CLOVES
Dried cloves of garlic may have a white, pink, or violet skin, depending on variety.

oniony herbs

CHIVES

Allium schoenoprasum

TASTING NOTES

All parts of chives have a light, onion aroma and a spicy, onion flavor.

This smallest and most delicately flavored member of the onion family originated in northern temperate zones. Chives have long grown wild all over Europe and North America, but widespread cultivation in Europe does not seem to have begun until the later Middle Ages. The herb became popular only in the 19th century.

PARTS USED

Stems and flowers.

BUYING AND STORING

Buy a clump from a nursery and divide the small bulbs as needed to guarantee a sufficient supply. Drying chives is pointless, but chopped and frozen they retain their flavor tolerably well and can be used straight from the freezer.

GROW YOUR OWN

Chives grow as grass-like clumps of hollow, bright green stems, with small, spherical, pink to purple flowerheads. They are perennials, easy to grow in any garden soil, but they must be watered well because the small bulbous roots remain very near the surface. Propagate by division. The plants die back in winter, but reappear very early in spring. They should be cut, not pulled, preferably the outer ones first to keep the clump neat. Always leave some top growth on the clumps to preserve the strength of the bulbs.

Culinary uses

Chives should never be cooked, since cooking quickly dissipates their taste. Chopped with a knife or with scissors, they can be added in generous measure to many dishes and salads. Their delicate onion flavor, crunchy texture, and fresh green appearance livens up potato salad and many a soup, and lends an equally upbeat note to any herb sauce. It has become traditional to serve chives with butter or sour cream as a dressing for baked potatoes. Stirred into thick yogurt, chives make a fresh relish for grilled fish. The attractive, bright flowers have a pleasant, light, onion taste and look good scattered over herb salads or added to omelettes.

Essential to fines herbes.

Good with avocados, cream cheese, egg dishes, fish and seafood, potatoes, smoked salmon, root vegetables, zucchini.

Combines well with basil, chervil, cilantro, fennel, paprika, parsley, sweet cicely, tarragon.

Fresh stems

Chives should be crisp, not floppy. Use quickly after cutting.

GARLIC CHIVES

Allium tuberosum

TASTING NOTES

Leaves and flowers have a stronger, more distinct garlic taste than those of ordinary chives; blanched leaves are milder. The taste is stronger in the flowers than in the leaves.

PARTS USED

Leaves and flowerbuds.

BUYING AND STORING

Specialty markets sell the chives in bundles, and blanched chives and the stiff flowerbud stems in smaller bundles. Once cut, chives wilt quickly – blanched garlic chives fastest of all. Green chives will keep for a few days in a plastic bag in the refrigerator, but the smell is strong.

GROW YOUR OWN

Garlic chives are robust; in warm climates they stay green all winter. The plants are taller than ordinary chives but tend to form neater and smaller clumps. They do not produce real bulbs and propagation is by the rhizome. Leaves can be cut for use at any time. Sometimes the plants are cut back and kept in the dark: the pale yellow shoots produced by this blanching are a prized delicacy. Flowers are harvested as buds, on the stems.

Garlic or Chinese chives are native to central and northern Asia, but grow also in subtropical China, India, and Indonesia. Records of the use of chives in China go back thousands of years. The plants have flat leaves rather than the hollow stems of ordinary chives, and the star-like flowers are white.

Culinary uses

Cut into short lengths, garlic chives can be quickly blanched to accompany pork or poultry. They are used in spring rolls and added at the last minute for pungency in stir-fried dishes of beef, shrimp, tofu, and many vegetables. Little bundles can be dipped in batter and deep-fried. The flowerbuds, sold separately on their stems, are a much-prized vegetable. In China and Japan, the flowers are ground and salted to make a spice. Blanched chives are a popular but expensive delicacy; they are stirred into soups, noodle dishes, and steamed vegetables at the last minute. Flower stems and leaves of garlic chives placed inside a bottle of white wine vinegar soon give it a light garlic flavor.

Leaves and flower stems
Bright green leaves, pale, blanched leaves, and bud stems are sold in specialty markets.

CELERY

Apium graveolens

Wild celery is an ancient European plant from which garden celery and celery root were bred in the 17th century. Cutting or leaf celery, also called smallage, resembles the original wild celery. Chinese celery is mid-green with leaves similar to those of garden celery.

Culinary uses

Cutting celery is used in Holland and Belgium rather as we use parsley, as a garnish or stirred into dishes just before serving. It is one of the herbs used for the traditional dish of eel in green sauce. In France, it is sold as a soup herb; in Greece, it is popular in fish and meat casseroles. Pick leaves to add to soups, stews, bouquets garnis instead of using a celery stick.

Chinese celery is used as a flavoring and as a vegetable. It is rarely eaten raw. Stalks are sliced and used in stir-fried dishes; leaves and stalks flavor soups, braised dishes, rice, and noodles throughout Southeast Asia. I have also enjoyed a very good Thai dish of fish steamed with Chinese celery.

Garden celery and celery root are eaten raw or cooked as vegetables, but you can also use their leaves as a flavoring.

Indian cooks also pair celery seed with tomato in curries. Try seeds in potato salad, in cabbage dishes, in stews, and in breads. The flavor is strong, so use sparingly.

Good with cabbage, chicken, cucumber, fish, potatoes, rice, soy sauce, tomatoes, tofu.

Combines well with cilantro, cloves, cumin, ginger, mustard, parsley, pepper, turmeric.

Cutting celery
A. graveolens

Cutting celery looks like a dark green, glossy version of flat-leaf parsley.

SEEDS
Seeds are added to soups in Scandinavia; crush a few to add to winter vegetable salads.

LOVAGE

Levisticum officinale

Lovage is native to western Asia and southern Europe, where it has been used since Roman times. Wild and cultivated forms are indistinguishable, and the herb has long been naturalized elsewhere – even in Australia. The Pilgrim Fathers are believed to have taken lovage to North America.

Culinary uses

Lovage can be used as celery or parsley, but is much stronger than either of these and should be used with caution. Its pungency diminishes in cooking.

Leaves, chopped stems, and roots work well in casseroles, soups, and stews. Leaves make a simple soup, alone or with potato or carrot and are often used in seafood chowders. They also liven up bean and creamy baked vegetable dishes. Add to a potato and rutabaga gratin or make potato cakes with lovage and Cheddar.
Good with apples, carrots, corn, cream cheese, egg dishes, ham, lamb, legumes, mushrooms, onions, pork, potatoes and other root vegetables, rice, smoked fish, tomatoes, tuna, zucchini.
Combines well with bay, caraway, chili, chives, dill, garlic, juniper, oregano, parsley, thyme.

TASTING NOTES

Lovage is strongly aromatic, somewhat similar to celery (in French it is called *céleri bâtard*, or false celery) but more pungent, with musky overtones and notes of anise, lemon, and yeast. The aroma and taste are distinct and tenacious.

PARTS USED

Leaves, stems, roots, seeds.

BUYING AND STORING

Seeds and ground, dried roots can be bought from some spice merchants. Cut lovage is seldom sold, but it is easy to grow your own; buy seeds or plants from an herb nursery. Pick leaves at any time; in a plastic bag they will keep for 3–4 days in the refrigerator. Cut off stems at the base, the outer ones first. As the seeds turn brown, pick fruiting stems and hang upside-down to dry, with a paper bag over the seedheads. These will keep for a year or two.

GROW YOUR OWN

This perennial herb can be grown from seed or by division. It does equally well in shade or sun, but its deep roots need moist, fertile, well-drained soil. The plant dies down in winter but is extremely hardy.

FRESH STEMS
Lovage is a tall, stately umbellifer with rather large, dark-green, toothed leaves and ridged, hollow stems.

bitter or astringent herbs

HYSSOP

Hyssopus officinalis

Hyssop has a strong and pleasant aroma of camphor and mint. The taste of the dark green leaves is refreshing but potent, hot, minty, and bitterish – reminiscent of rosemary, savory, and thyme.

Hyssop is a low, perennial shrub, semi-woody and semi-evergreen, that is native to northern Africa, southern Europe, and western Asia. It is a handsome, compact plant that has long been naturalized in central and western Europe. The Romans used it as a base for an herbal wine, and it was cultivated as a condiment and a strewing herb in monastic gardens during the early Middle Ages.

PARTS USED

Leaves and young shoots; flowers.

BUYING AND STORING

In a plastic bag in the vegetable crisper of the refrigerator hyssop will keep for about a week.

GROW YOUR OWN

Hyssop grows well from seed but can also be divided or propagated by cuttings. It likes dry, rocky, well-drained soils, needs sun but tolerates shade. Every 3 years or so, hyssop plants should be divided or they will become too woody. As hyssop is virtually evergreen, its leaves can be picked nearly year-round. The long, dense flowerspikes that appear in late summer are attractive to bees. Their color depends on the variety grown: *H. o. albus* has white flowers; *H .o.* subsp. *aristatus*, dark blue ones; *H. o. roseus*, pink.

Culinary uses

Hyssop leaves and young shoots can be used in salads (to which the flowers can make a robust garnish) or added to soups. The herb is particularly good in rabbit, kid, and game stews; rubbing it onto fatty meats such as lamb can make them easier to digest. It has long been used to flavor non-alcoholic summer drinks, digestives, and liqueurs. It is very good in fruit pies and compotes, and with sherbets and desserts made using assertively flavored fruits such as apricots, morello cherries, peaches, and raspberries. A sugar syrup made for a fruit dish will benefit from boiling with a sprig of hyssop.

Good with apricots, beets, cabbage, carrots, egg dishes, game, legumes, mushrooms, peaches, winter squashes.
Combines well with bay, chervil, mint, parsley, thyme.

Fresh sprigs
Hyssop should be used sparingly or it will overwhelm other flavors.

LEAVES
Both leaves and flowers retain much of their strength when dried. The tiny flowers have a more delicate flavor than the leaves.

CHICORY
Cichorium intybus

Chicory is a tall herbaceous perennial, native to the Mediterranean basin and Asia Minor. The modern cultivated forms originated in 16th-century Europe. In time they gave rise to two very different forced forms: in the late 18th century the Dutch grew the roots for use as a cheaper substitute for coffee – as an additive without caffeine it remains popular in Belgium, France, Germany, and the US; in 1845, the Belgians developed the blanched form grown under soil or sawdust that we still know as Belgian endive or witloof.

TASTING NOTES

Chicory has no smell. It has a milky white juice containing inulin, which accounts for the bitter taste – quite pleasant in the crisp, young leaves but harsh in old ones. The flowers are not at all bitter.

PARTS USED

Young green leaves; flowers.

BUYING AND STORING

Seeds and plants can usually be bought from an herb nursery. Leaves will keep in a plastic bag in the vegetable crisper of the refrigerator for 2–3 days. Flowers need to be used immediately.

GROW YOUR OWN

Chicory is easily grown from seed in almost any water-retentive but reasonably well-drained soil that allows penetration by the very long taproots. The light green leaves are large at the base, smaller on the upper, branching stems. The large, light blue, daisy-like flowers, which last only a day or so and close in the midday sun, appear all through the summer and early autumn. Suppressing the flower stems early encourages leaf growth.

Culinary uses

Young leaves are used in salads; the edible flowers can also be added to salads as cheerful decoration. Older leaves benefit from quick blanching and are then used in cooked dishes – they are not appetizing in salads.

Good with fresh cheeses, lettuce and other salad greens, nuts.

Combines well with chervil, cilantro, cresses, parsley, purslane, salad burnet, sweet cicely.

Fresh leaves
Chicory grows wild in much of Europe and North America. In the garden it can reach 3⅓ft (1m) or more by flowering time.

OREGANO AND MARJORAM
Origanum species

Low, bushy perennials of the mint family, the marjorams and oreganos are native to the Mediterranean and western Asia. The plants are often confused, partly because marjoram used to have its own genus, *Majorana*, but also because the word "oregano" is often used simply as a term for a certain type of flavor and aroma. Thus, unrelated plants with a similar aromatic profile may also be called oregano.

Common oregano
O. vulgare

This plant has reddish stems that are slightly woody; the leaves are mid-green and hairy underneath; the flowers deep pink, white, or mauve.

DRIED LEAVES
Dried marjoram and oregano are more intensely aromatic than fresh and have a stronger flavor. Several varieties of oregano are sold dried under the Greek name rigani.

Culinary uses

Oregano has become an essential ingredient in much Italian cooking, especially for pasta sauces, pizza, and roasted vegetables. For the Greeks it is the favorite herb for souvlaki, baked fish, and Greek salad. In Mexico, it is a key flavoring for bean dishes, burrito and taco fillings, and salsas. Throughout Spain and Latin America, it is used for meat stews and roasts, soups, and baked vegetables. Combined with paprika, cumin, and chili powder it flavors Tex-Mex chile con carne and other meat stews. Its strong flavor works well with grills and in stuffings, hearty soups, marinades, vegetable stews, even hamburgers. It will also flavor oils and vinegars.

The more delicate flavor of marjoram is easily lost in cooking, so it should be added only at the last moment. It is good in salads, egg dishes, and mushroom sauces, with fish and poultry. It makes more delicate stuffings than oregano. Fresh, it makes a great sorbet. Use leaves and flowerknots in salads, and with mozzarella and other young cheeses.

Sprigs of either marjoram or oregano placed on the coals of a grill give a fine flavor to whatever is cooked on top.

Good with anchovies, artichokes, beans, cabbage, carrots, cauliflower, cheese dishes, chicken, corn, duck, eggplant, eggs, fish and shellfish, lamb, mushrooms, onions, pork, potatoes, poultry, spinach, squash, sweet peppers, tomatoes, veal, venison.

Combines well with basil, bay, chili, cumin, garlic, paprika, parsley, rosemary, sage, sumac, (lemon) thyme.

Sweet marjoram *O. majorana*

This pretty plant, also called knotted marjoram, has gray-green, slightly hairy leaves and clusters of white flowers. Its taste is more delicate and somewhat sweeter than that of common oregano and it does not lend itself to long cooking.

pungent and spicy **herbs**

ROSEMARY

Rosmarinus officinalis

Rosemary is a dense, woody, evergreen perennial, native to the Mediterranean but long cultivated in temperate zones throughout Europe and America. It has been grown in England since Roman times. In the early 9th century, Charlemagne, in his *Capitulaire de Villes*, included it in the list of essential plants to be grown on the imperial estates; in the later Middle Ages it was still used as a strewing or incense herb.

Fresh leaves
Rosemary leaves can be tough, so they are best chopped before being added to any dish in which they will be eaten.

Culinary uses

The flavor of rosemary is strong and unsubtle; it is not diminished by long cooking, so use rosemary judiciously, even in slow-cooked stews. In Mediterranean cuisines it is much used with vegetables fried in olive oil; in Italy, it is popular with veal. Whole sprigs are good in marinades, especially for lamb, and will give a subtle, smoky flavor when placed under meat or poultry being grilled or roasted. Older, stronger stems can be used as skewers for kebabs, or as basting brushes. Rosemary is very good in cookies and crackers, and in focaccia and other breads. Young sprigs can be used to flavor olive oil, infused in milk, cream, or syrup for desserts, or steeped for summer drinks such as lemonade. Flowers frozen in ice cubes make a pretty garnish for such drinks. Crystallized rosemary flowers are pretty, but quite fiddly to make.

Essential to herbes de Provence.

Good with apricots, cabbage, cream cheese, eggplant, eggs, fish, lamb, lentils, mushrooms, onions, oranges, parsnips, pork, potatoes, poultry, rabbit, tomatoes, veal, winter squashes.

Combines well with bay, chives, garlic, lavender, lovage, mint, oregano, parsley, sage, savory, thyme.

Herbes de Provence

Used with meat, game, vegetable, and tomato dishes, this herb blend can be fresh or dried. This version includes rosemary, thyme, marjoram, savory, and bay.

SAGE
Salvia species

Sage can be mild, musky, and balsamic, or strongly camphorous with astringent notes and a warm spiciness. Generally, variegated species are milder than common sage. Dried sage is more potent than fresh and can be acrid and musty; it is best avoided, except for tea.

PARTS USED

Leaves, fresh or dried. All sages have attractive, hooded flowers that make pretty garnishes.

BUYING AND STORING

Fresh sage leaves are best picked and used as soon as possible. If you buy them, wrap them in paper towel and keep in the salad crisper of the refrigerator for no more than a few days. Dried sage will keep for up to 6 months if stored away from light in an airtight container.

GROW YOUR OWN

Sage does best on warm, dry soils. Its aromatic strength varies according to soil and climate. Leaves can be harvested from spring to autumn. Plants are best cut back after flowering. Purple, variegated, and tricolor sages (*p.61*) are less hardy than common sage, and pineapple sage needs protection from freezing temperatures.

The sages are native to the north Mediterranean and are mostly perennial, shrubby plants that thrive on warm, dry soils. The great variety of their textured, velvety foliage – from pale gray-green to green splashed with silver or gold, as well as the dark leaves of purple sage – makes them attractive garden plants as well as an invaluable addition to the cook's repertoire of seasonings.

Common sage *S. officinalis*

There are broad and narrow-leaved varieties of common sage. Young, green leaves are less pungent than the older, gray ones. Narrow-leaved sage has pretty lilac, blue, or white flowers. Broad-leaved sage seldom flowers.

Culinary uses

Sage aids the digestion of fatty and oily foods and is traditionally used as a partner for them. In Britain, sage is associated with pork, goose, and duck, and works well in stuffings for these meats. In the US, sage and onion stuffing is often used for the Thanksgiving turkey. Sage also makes an excellent flavoring for pork sausages, and in Germany it accompanies eel. The Greeks use it in meat stews and with poultry, and also in a tea. Italians use sage with liver and veal (saltimbocca alla romana is the classic dish), and to flavor focaccia and polenta; they make a well-flavored pasta sauce by gently heating a few leaves in butter. Sage is not a subtle herb, so use sparingly.

Good with apples, dried beans, cheese, onions, tomatoes.

Combines well with bay, caraway, cutting celery, dried ginger, lovage, marjoram, paprika, parsley, savory, thyme.

Purple sage

S. o. Purpurascens Group

This sage has musky, spicy tones and is slightly less pungent than common sage. It rarely flowers, but when it does the blue flowers look stunning against the foliage.

Bouquet garni for meats

Little bundles of herbs such as this can be varied to suit the dish to be cooked. Sprigs of thyme, sage, cutting celery, and parsley make a fine flavoring for stews.

THYME

Thymus species

The whole plant has a warm, earthy, and peppery fragrance when lightly brushed. The taste is spicy, with notes of cloves and mint, a hint of camphor, and a mouth-cleansing aftertaste.

Thyme is a small, hardy, evergreen shrub with small, aromatic leaves, indigenous to the Mediterranean basin. It grows wild on the hot, arid hillsides of its native region, where it has infinitely more flavor than it ever achieves in cooler regions. Wild thyme tends to be woody and straggly. Cultivated varieties have more tender stems and a bushy form; there are hundreds of them, each with a slightly different aroma, and they have a tendency to cross-breed as well.

Common thyme T. vulgaris

The basic thyme for cooking, also called garden thyme, is a cultivated variety of wild Mediterranean thyme. It forms a sturdy, upright shrub with gray-green leaves and white or pale lilac flowers. There are a number of garden thymes, including English "broad-leaf" and French "narrow-leaf" varieties.

PARTS USED

Leaves and sprigs; flowers for garnishes.

BUYING AND STORING

Many varieties of thyme are sold by nurseries, but make sure they smell when brushed lightly by hand. Common and lemon thyme are available fresh from supermarkets. Fresh leaves will keep for up to a week stored in a plastic bag in the refrigerator. Dried thyme will retain its flavor through the winter.

GROW YOUR OWN

All thymes need very well-drained, sandy soil and as much sun as they can get. They benefit from the heat reflected off patio stone paving and the rocks in rock gardens. Propagation is easiest by division. Pick leaves when needed – the more often the better, or the plant may become straggly and woody. Harvest thyme for drying just before it flowers.

Culinary uses

Thyme is an essential flavoring in much Western and Middle-Eastern cooking. Unlike most herbs, it withstands long, slow cooking; used with discretion it enhances other herbs without overpowering them, and in stews and casseroles combines well with onions, beer, or red wine. Thyme has become indispensable in every French stew, from pot-au-feu to cassoulet, but equally in Spanish ones and, by extension, those of Mexico and Latin America, where it is often used in combination with chili peppers. It is widely used to flavor pâtés, thick vegetable soups, tomato and wine-based sauces, and in marinades for pork and game. In Britain, it is used in stuffings, pies, and jugged hare. The dried herb is essential in the Creole and Cajun cooking of Louisiana, where it appears in gumbos and jambalayas; elsewhere in the US, fresh thyme is used as a traditional flavoring in New England clam chowder.

Essential to most bouquets garnis.

Good with cabbage, carrots, corn, eggplant, lamb, leeks, legumes, onions, potatoes, rabbit, tomatoes, wild mushrooms.

Combines well with allspice, basil, bay, chili, clove, garlic, lavender, marjoram, nutmeg, oregano, paprika, parsley, rosemary, savory.

Lemon thyme *T. citriodorus*

This is a compact, upright shrub with mauve-pink flowers that gives a fresh lemony note to fish and seafood, roast chicken, or veal; it can be used in cookies, breads, and fruit salads. For the cook lemon thyme is the most important variety after garden thyme.

SAVORY
Satureja species

Highly aromatic, as the name suggests, savory was one of the strongest flavorings available before spices reached Europe. Summer savory (*S. hortensis*) is native to the eastern Mediterranean and the Caucasus; winter savory (*S. montana*) to southern Europe, Turkey, and North Africa. Both were taken to northern Europe by the Romans and to North America by early settlers.

PARTS USED

Leaves and sprigs; flowers for garnishes and salads.

BUYING AND STORING

Savory is not available as a cut herb, but plants are available from nurseries. Summer savory will keep for 5–6 days, winter savory for up to 10 days, in a plastic bag in the refrigerator. Savory retains its flavor well if frozen, chopped or as sprigs. To dry summer savory, hang the stems in an airy, dark place.

GROW YOUR OWN

Summer savory is an annual, winter savory an evergreen perennial. Both can be grown from seed, and winter savory can be propagated by division in spring. Both prefer light, well-drained soils and full sun. Summer savory does best in a rich soil; cut back on flowering to encourage new growth. Winter savory will grow in poorer soils.

Summer savory
S. hortensis

This savory is a slender plant with soft, grayish leaves and white or pinkish flowers. Summer savory leaves are tender, whereas those of winter savory are tough.

FRESH SPRIGS
The leaves have the most intense aroma if harvested just before flowering.

Culinary uses

Because they are pungent, both savories are good flavorings for long-cooked meat and vegetable dishes and stuffings. Savory is frequently associated with beans, as its German name Bohnenkraut (bean herb) indicates. Summer savory is best with green and fava beans, whereas either can be used with white beans and other legumes. Savory is also good with cabbage, root vegetables, and onions, and reduces their strong cooking smells.

Summer savory is often added to bouquets garnis for lamb, pork, and game dishes. It is also good with oil-rich fish such as eel and mackerel. Chopped finely, it can be added to salads; it is especially good with potato, bean, and lentil salads.

Winter savory (called poivre d'âne or pebre d'aï – donkey pepper – in Provence, France) is more widely used around the Mediterranean. Chopped leaves and flowers are added to soups, fish stews, frittate, pizza, rabbit, and lamb dishes. It is also used to coat Banon, a Provençal goat or sheep milk cheese.

Good with beans, beets, cabbage, cheese, eggs, fish, legumes, potatoes, rabbit, sweet peppers, tomatoes.

Combines well with basil, bay, cumin, garlic, lavender, marjoram, mint, oregano, parsley, rosemary, thyme.

Winter savory *S. montana*

This is a woody, compact shrub with stiff, glossy, ark green leaves and lavender or white flowers. Although the savories can be used interchangeably to some extent, both should be used judiciously, and winter savory in much smaller amounts than summer savory.

FRESH SPRIGS
Winter savory leaves can be harvested year-round.

CILANTRO

Coriandrum sativum

TASTING NOTES

Leaves, roots, and unripe seeds all have the same aroma. Some people are addicted to its refreshing, lemony-ginger aroma with notes of sage; others hate it and find it soapy and disagreeable. The flavor is delicate yet complex, with a suggestion of pepper, mint, and lemon.

PARTS USED

Leaves and sprigs, roots.

BUYING AND STORING

Cilantro is available from specialty markets and supermarkets; bunches are sold with roots intact in Asian markets, or you can grow your own. In a plastic bag, cilantro will keep for 3–4 days in the refrigerator vegetable crisper. Frozen cilantro retains its flavor fairly well; chop and freeze in small pots or in ice-cube trays covered with a little water. Dried cilantro is not worthwhile and is never used in Asian cuisines.

GROW YOUR OWN

Coriander is an annual that grows easily from seed in a warm, sunny spot. Leaves can be gathered throughout the growing season. Clusters of small, white or pinkish flowers produce the seeds. Seeds should be harvested when fully ripe; to dry them, hang bunches of stems in a warm place and put a paper bag over the seedheads.

Native to the Mediterranean and western Asia, coriander is now grown worldwide. It is both herb and spice, and a fragrant staple in many cuisines. The fresh leaves, commonly called cilantro, are essential to Asian, Latin American, and Portuguese cooking. Thai cooks also use the thin, spindly root. In Western cooking the fruit or seed is used as a spice; in the Middle East and India, both are common in the kitchen. Another name for the herb is Chinese parsley.

Fresh sprigs
Cilantro was called a "very stinking herbe" by Gerard, the 16th-century herbalist, and is known as the "fragrant plant" by the Chinese. The herb's aroma continues to provoke both dislike and enthusiasm today.

ROOTS
The roots are more pungent and musky than the leaves, with a light, citrus smell.

Culinary uses

Except when they are used in a curry or similar paste, cilantro leaves are always added at the end of cooking; high or prolonged heat reduces their flavor. Cilantro leaves are used lavishly throughout most of Asia, in delicately flavored soups, in stir-fried dishes with ginger and scallions, in curries and braised dishes. Thai cooks use the roots for curry pastes and combine leaves with basil, mint, and chili peppers.

In India, cilantro garnishes many savory dishes and is combined with other herbs and spices in green masala pastes. India and Mexico share a liking for cilantro with green chili peppers in chutneys, relishes, and salsas. Mexicans also combine cilantro and chilies with garlic and lime juice to make a dressing for vegetables, or for a sauce in which to cook fish.

In Bolivia and Peru, cilantro, chilies, and huacatay flavor a very assertive table sauce. In the Middle East, cilantro is essential to Yemeni zhug and hilbeh, both pungent spice pastes, and is combined with nuts and spices, lemon juice, and olive oil to make flavoring mixtures.

The Portuguese are the only Europeans who have continued to use cilantro to the same extent as it was used in the 16th century. They partner it with potatoes and fava beans, and with their excellent clams.

Essential to hilbeh, zhug, chermoula, ceviche, guacamole.

Good with avocados, coconut milk, corn, cucumber, fish and seafood, legumes, lemons and limes, rice, root vegetables.

Combines well with basil, chili, chives, dill, galangal, garlic, ginger, lemon grass, mint, parsley.

Yemeni zhug paste

This mixture of cilantro, hot chili peppers, garlic, cumin, and cardamom is used as a condiment.

ARUGULA

Eruca vesicaria subsp. sativa

TASTING NOTES

Arugula's toothed leaves have a warm, peppery smell that rises from the bed as soon as the first leaf is picked. The taste is pleasantly pungent. The small, white or yellow, edible flowers have a faint orange aroma; they make an attractive garnish.

PARTS USED

Leaves and flowers.

BUYING AND STORING

Arugula is now readily available in supermarkets, either on its own or in bags of mixed salad leaves. All the same it is well worth growing from seed, as it needs no looking after and is at its best freshly picked. It can be stored in a plastic bag in the refrigerator vegetable crisper for a few days. Drying arugula is a waste of time, nor does it freeze well, but as fresh leaves can be obtained easily this matters little.

GROW YOUR OWN

Arugula and wild arugula are both very easy to grow from seed, and staggered sowing will give a useful crop virtually throughout the year. They thrive in partial shade. Arugula is an annual, wild arugula a perennial; both self-seed only too readily. Leaves are ready for picking in 6–8 weeks.

Arugula is native to Asia and southern Europe and naturalized in North America. It was a popular herb in Europe until the 18th century, when it virtually disappeared everywhere but in Italy. After nearly two centuries of neglect it is having a well-deserved revival, and is currently the most fashionable salad herb in both the US and Europe (where it is variously known as rucola, roquette, and rocket).

Culinary uses

Whole leaves can be added to any salad of mixed leaves or potato salad, or will make a strongly flavored salad on their own, especially with a nut oil dressing. Arugula leaves can also be used as a fragrant bed on which to present other salads, poached eggs, or roasted sweet red peppers. Arugula and prosciutto makes a good sandwich filling, and with mushrooms or cheese a filling for ravioli. Shredded leaves are good in herb butter for seafood or herb dressings, especially for pasta. Arugula can also be used to make pesto, with or without basil.

Good with goat cheese, lettuce, potatoes, salad herbs, tomato.

Combines well with basil, borage, cilantro, cresses, dill, lovage, mint, parsley, salad burnet.

Arugula *E. v. subsp. sativa*

The leaves become progressively more peppery the longer they stay on the plant, but once the flowers fully develop their taste diminishes.

Wild arugula
Diplotaxis muralis

Wild arugula has narrower, more sharply toothed leaves and a more peppery taste than its cultivated counterpart. It can be bought as growing plants from herb nurseries or specialist suppliers.

Turkish arugula *Bunias orientalis*

Turkish arugula grows wild in parts of Asia. It has a sharp and coarse flavor, rather like horseradish, and a tinge of sulfur. Called rokka, it can often be bought in large bunches from Turkish markets. It is better cooked, for instance in a vegetable frittata, than used raw.

WASABI
Eutrema wasabi

This herbaceous perennial grows primarily in cold mountain streams in Japan; recently some cultivation has started in California and New Zealand. The name translates as mountain hollyhock. In the West the plant is sometimes called Japanese horseradish, a reference to its pungency and the fact that the gnarled and knobby root, on average about 4–5in (10–12cm) long, is the edible part.

PARTS USED

Roots.

BUYING AND STORING

Some specialty produce markets sell fresh wasabi, but more usually it is sold either in tubes as a paste or in cans as powder. Fresh wasabi will keep for a week, wrapped in plastic wrap, in the vegetable crisper of the refrigerator. Powdered wasabi has a shelf life of several months but can develop a rather stale aftertaste. Tubes of paste must be refrigerated after opening. The paste loses its potency more quickly than the powder.

HARVESTING

Wasabi can only be cultivated in cold, pure, running water; commercial growing is normally done in flooded terraces, usually in partial shade. It is very expensive to produce.

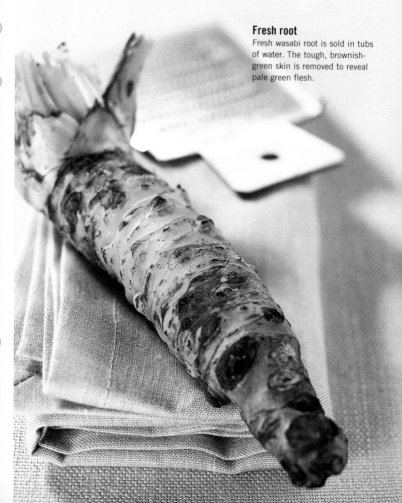

Fresh root
Fresh wasabi root is sold in tubs of water. The tough, brownish-green skin is removed to reveal pale green flesh.

Culinary uses

Wasabi does not retain its flavor when cooked, so it is generally served with or added to cold food. In Japan, it accompanies most raw fish dishes. Sashimi and sushi plates always have a tiny mound of grated wasabi or wasabi paste, which is then mixed to individual taste with a soy dipping sauce. In sushi it often appears as an ingredient as well as a garnish, between raw fish and the vinegared rice. With soy sauce and dashi (soup stock), wasabi makes the popular wasabi-joyu sauce. On its own, wasabi can be used to give a sharp piquancy to dressings and marinades. It also makes a good butter that keeps in the refrigerator for weeks; this makes an interesting change served on filet mignon or other steaks.

Essential to sashimi, sushi.
Good with avocado, beef, raw fish, rice, seafood.
Combines well with ginger, soy sauce.

GRATED ROOT
In Japan, peeled wasabi root is grated finely on an oroshigane, a flat grater tightly set with thin spikes. Made of stainless steel, tinned copper, or plastic, these can be bought from Japanese stores.

WASABI PASTE
Because wasabi is so expensive, harsher-tasting horseradish mixed with mustard and green coloring is frequently passed off as wasabi paste or powder. Real paste costs twice as much as fake and has a shorter shelf life.

HORSERADISH
Armoracia rusticana

Horseradish root is very pungent and mustard-like when just grated, enough to make your eyes water and your nose run. The taste is acrid, sharp, and hot. The leaves are also pungent when crushed; the taste is sharp, but much milder than that of the root.

PARTS USED

Fresh young leaves; fresh or dried roots.

BUYING AND STORING

Fresh roots are sold in supermarkets, particularly near Passover (horseradish is one of the five bitter herbs of the Seder). Fresh roots taken from the garden will keep for months in dry sand, bought ones for 2–3 weeks in a plastic bag in the refrigerator, even after being cut and part-used. Grated horseradish can be frozen. Dried roots can be bought powdered or flaked.

GROW YOUR OWN

Horseradish is propagated from root cuttings. It grows very easily in sandy loam soil with good drainage, but is invasive – the tiniest bit left in the soil will be enough to overrun a patch, so plant in a container, as one does mint. The roots can be lifted throughout the winter, if the ground is not frozen.

Horseradish is a perennial native to eastern Europe and western Asia, where it still grows wild in the steppes of Russia and the Ukraine. Its culinary use probably originated in Russia and eastern Europe, spreading to central Europe in the early Middle Ages, later to Scandinavia and western Europe. English settlers took it to North America, and cultivation was established by German and eastern European immigrants around 1850. By about 1860, bottled horseradish was available as one of the first convenience condiments.

Fresh root
Slicing a long, thick, hairy, yellowish-brown horseradish root reveals white flesh. Grating releases its highly pungent volatile oil, but this dissipates very quickly and does not survive cooking.

Culinary uses

Freshly grated horseradish can be stabilized with a little lemon juice. It is good on salads of potatoes or root vegetables, and aids the digestion of oily fish. A traditional accompaniment to roast beef – and to tongue in Germany – it also goes well with boiled beef. Why it is served with oysters – often alongside tomato ketchup and Tabasco sauce – is a mystery to me, since it masks the oysters' flavor completely.

Horseradish is easily made into a sauce by blending it with cream and vinegar, or with sour cream alone, with or without sugar. A popular Austrian condiment is Apfelkren, made by mixing horseradish with grated apples and a little lemon juice. With apricot preserve and a little mustard, horseradish makes a good glaze for ham. Mixed with mustard into butter it is good with corn-on-the-cob or carrots. A few tender, young leaves will give a

pleasant, sharp taste to a green salad. Processed horseradish browns as it ages and loses its strength. Many condiments have too much added sugar, which masks the fresh and pungent flavor.

Good with apple, avocado, baked ham, beef, beets, oily or smoked fish, potatoes, pork sausages, seafood.

Combines well with capers, celery, chives, cream, dill, mustard, tomato paste, vinegar, yogurt.

GRATED ROOT
Sprinkle lemon juice on grated horseradish to preserve its white color and pungency. Vinegar is used to prevent browning and loss of flavor in commercial horseradish condiments.

EPAZOTE

Chenopodium ambrosioides

Not everyone likes epazote. The aroma is described as that of turpentine or putty by those who hate it, while it reminds others of savory, mint, and citrus. I think of it as camphorous, earthy, and minty. The taste is pungent and refreshing, bitterish with lingering citrus notes and a curious, oddly addictive rankness.

PARTS USED

Leaves, fresh or dried.

BUYING AND STORING

It is difficult to obtain fresh epazote, except in Latin markets, unless you grow it yourself; dried epazote has much less taste but is still good in cooking. Make sure you get the leaves, not the stems, which are also sold dried – these are fine for tea but less good in cooking.

GROW YOUR OWN

Epazote can easily be grown from seed in dry soil. Its flavor will depend on the amount of sun it gets – in colder climates it is less aromatic. It is an annual but will reseed itself only too readily. Once established, it should be possible to overwinter plants indoors.

Native to central and southern Mexico, epazote was an essential ingredient of Mayan cuisine in the Yucatán and Guatemala. It is now widely cultivated and used in southern Mexico, the northern countries of South America, and the Caribbean islands. Its use is spreading in North America, where it is often found as a weed along roadsides and in towns; it is grown commercially in the south. It still has to make its mark in Europe, although it grows wild there also.

Culinary uses

The fresh herb is commonly used in Mexican bean dishes, partly for its flavor and partly because it reduces flatulence. Chopped finely, it is used in soups and stews. Although used raw in salsas, its flavor works best in cooking; add for only the last 15 minutes or so to avoid bitterness. It is essential to mole verde, a green cooking sauce of tomatillos and green chili peppers, thickened with nuts or seeds. Use epazote lightly: it easily overwhelms other flavors, and in larger doses it is somewhat toxic and can cause dizziness.

Essential to black bean dishes, mole verde, quesadillas, salsas.

Good with chorizo, corn, fish and shellfish, green vegetables, legumes, lime, mushrooms, onion, pork, rice, squash, sweet peppers, tomatillos, white cheese.

Combines well with chili, cilantro, cloves, cumin, garlic, oregano.

Fresh leaves
The taste of epazote is too pungent for many people. Its name, deriving from Nahuatl, an Aztec language still spoken around Mexico City, refers to a disagreeable odor – *epatl* means skunk and *tzotl* sweat.

DRIED LEAVES
Use dried leaves only when fresh are unavailable.

MUGWORT
Artemisia vulgaris

TASTING NOTES

The aroma of mugwort is of juniper and pepper, lightly pungent with a hint of mint and sweetness. The flavor is similar, with a mild, bitter aftertaste.

Mugwort is an herbaceous perennial that grows wild in many habitats throughout most of North and South America, Europe, and Asia. In the Middle Ages, it was used instead of hops as a bittering agent in brewing beer. In the 18th century, it was one of the most used kitchen herbs in Europe, but it has since gone out of fashion except in Germany, where it is popular as Gänsekraut, goose herb.

PARTS USED

Fresh young shoots; leaves and flowerbuds, both fresh and dried.

BUYING AND STORING

Buy plants from a nursery. Pick young leaves as needed. Flower stems are dried by hanging in a dark, warm place. This can take 3 weeks, or 4–6 hours if left in a warm oven. Once dry, buds and leaves can be stored in an airtight container for up to a year. Dried mugwort is available from Japanese markets.

GROW YOUR OWN

Mugwort is quite adaptable, but does prefer full sun and a rich, moist soil. It can be propagated from seed or by division of the rhizomes. It should be kept in check or it will run rampant. Numerous small, reddish-brown florets bloom in late summer and early autumn on panicled spikes. Harvest just before the flowerbuds open: the flowers can get unpleasantly bitter.

Culinary uses

Mugwort works well with oily fish, fatty meat, and poultry such as duck or goose, helping in their digestion. It is good in stuffings and marinades, and also flavors stock quite well. Its aroma develops with cooking, so it should be added early. It has no natural partners among herbs, but garlic and pepper go well with it. Called yomogi in Japan, it is used as a vegetable, as a popular ingredient in mochi (rice cakes), and as a seasoning for soba noodles. Young leaves are boiled or stir-fried thoughout Asia. Young leaves can also be shredded over a green salad or stirred into the dressing. Cider vinegar in which mugwort has been steeped for some weeks is good for salad dressings and marinades.

Good with beans, duck, eel, game, goose, onions, pork, rice.

Combines well with garlic, pepper.

Fresh leaves
Leaves are smooth and green on top, downy white underneath.

DRIED LEAVES
In Germany, mugwort is available fresh and dried; elsewhere it is necessary to grow your own, or buy dried via the internet.

preparing herbs

STRIPPING, CHOPPING, AND POUNDING HERBS

Some herbs – chives, chervil, and cilantro – have soft stems, but in most cases leaves must be stripped from the stems before being used. Small leaves and sprigs are used whole in salads or as a garnish, but most leaves are chopped, sliced, or pounded, depending on the dish being prepared. Chop, slice, or pound herbs just before you need them or their flavors will dissipate.

Stripping leaves

When stripping herbs you may find that you are not able to go right to the top of the stem because it is too tender and will break. Such upper stems are likely to be soft enough to chop with the leaves. Some herbs are easier to strip from the top down, particularly those with large leaves.

Stripping tough stems ▲
Hold the bottom of the stem firmly in one hand, place the thumb and first finger of the other hand on either side of the stem, and, using the thumb to guide, pull upward, stripping the leaves onto a board.

Stripping tender stems ▶
Strip fennel and dill from the bottom of the stem, pulling the leaf sprays upward with one hand. Take out any thick stems that remain and strip off the leaves.

Chopping leaves

Herbs are chopped according to the dish for which they are needed. Finely chopped herbs integrate well with other ingredients. They provide immediate flavor because so much of their surface is exposed, allowing the essential oils to blend into the food quickly, but they may lose their flavor in cooking. Coarsely chopped herbs keep their identity, flavor, and texture longer and survive cooking better than finely chopped herbs, but are less attractive in a smooth-textured dish.

Using a mezzaluna ▶

Some cooks prefer to use the curved mezzaluna for large amounts of herbs. This implement is rocked backward and forward to great effect. Herbs can also be chopped in the small bowl of a food processor: use the pulse button and chop briefly. Make sure the herbs are completely dry or they will turn out unattractively pastelike. It is more difficult to obtain uniformly chopped leaves in a processor.

① Choose a large, sharp knife for cutting herbs or you will bruise rather than cut them. Lay the herbs on a board, hold the point of the blade on the board with the flat fingers of your non-cutting hand, and chop up and down briskly in a rocking motion.

② Scoop the herbs back into a pile from time to time with the flat of the blade. Continue the chopping action until the herbs are cut as finely as you need.

Making a chiffonade

Any finely shredded vegetable used as a garnish is termed a "chiffonade." Shredded herb leaves make an attractive garnish and also keep their texture well in a sauce.

1 If using leaves such as sorrel, remove the thick vein from each one beforehand.

2 Stack a few similar-sized leaves one on top of the other and roll them up tightly.

3 ▶ Using a sharp knife, cut the roll of leaves into very fine slices.

Pounding herbs

Herbs can be pounded to a paste using a mortar and pestle, and garlic is easily puréed in a mortar with a little salt. A smoother result is achieved more quickly in a food processor.

1 ▲ Pesto is the classic pounded herb sauce. Start by pounding some basil and garlic in a large mortar.

2 ▶ Gradually work in some pine nuts, grated Parmesan, and olive oil, and mix to a paste.

DRYING AND RUBBING HERBS

Drying does not suit all herbs. Those with woody stems and tough leaves, such as thyme, rosemary, oregano, and lemon verbena, dry best and keep their flavor well, while those with soft leaves and stems, such as basil, parsley, chervil, and marjoram, lose their flavor almost completely. Mint is an exception: although it has soft leaves, it dries well. The traditional way to dry herbs is to hang them in bunches, but they also dry well in a microwave oven. For the best flavor, harvest herbs just before their flowerbuds open, when the essential oils are at their most concentrated, and pick early in the day.

Freezing herbs

Soft herbs that do not dry well can be frozen. Frozen herbs keep their fragrance for 3–4 months. Use for soups, stews, braised dishes, and sauces.

◀ Freezing chopped herbs
Wash and dry the herbs well, chop, and freeze in small pots or in ice-cube trays with a little water or oil. Store the cubes in plastic bags.

▲ Freezing puréed herbs
Alternatively, purée each herb with a little oil in a food processor and freeze in bags or plastic pots.

Drying herbs

Herbs hanging in a well-ventilated place will dry within a few days to a week. Those kept in a steamy kitchen will not dry well. Avoid direct sunlight or too much heat because they will cause the essential oils to evaporate.

Microwaving herbs ▷
Scatter two handfuls of cleaned leaves and sprigs evenly on a double layer of paper towel and microwave on high for 2½ minutes. Bay leaves may need a little longer. Microwaving preserves color well. Store as below.

① When preparing herbs for drying, remove any old or discolored leaves. Tie the herbs in small bunches and hang in a well-ventilated place out of direct sunlight, such as an attic or shed.

② Drying is complete when the leaves feel brittle. Large leaves or small flowerbuds can be rubbed between the palms of your hands to crumble them. Otherwise, strip the leaves from the stems. Store in airtight containers.

MAKING VINEGARS, OILS, AND BUTTERS

Flavored vinegars and oils are useful for sauces, dressings, and marinades, and for stirring into soups and stews just before serving. Basil, dill, garlic, lavender, lemon verbena, rosemary, tarragon, and thyme make excellent vinegars; among spices try chili peppers, peppercorns, and dill, fennel, mustard, or coriander seeds. For oils, try basil, bay, dill, garlic, mint, oregano, rosemary, savory, or thyme, or chili peppers and cumin, dill, or fennel seeds. Herb and spice butters provide a quick dressing for broiled or fried fish, poultry, and meat, and steamed or boiled vegetables, as well as a good sandwich spread.

Making herb vinegar or oil

Flavored vinegars will keep in a cool, dark place for several years, mellowing as they age. Oils will keep for up to 2 weeks and should be refrigerated.

1. To make an herb or spice vinegar, take about 2oz (60g) of herb sprigs or whole spices – about 1½ cups herb sprigs and 2–4 tbsp whole spices – and crush to bring out their flavor.

2. ◄ Put them into a large jar and cover with 2 cups (500ml) white wine vinegar, cider vinegar, or rice vinegar. Close the jar and let infuse for 2–3 weeks. Flavors will develop more quickly if the jar is placed in the sun.

3. Strain into bottles, add a fresh herb sprig or a few fresh spices to each one for decoration, close with a cork or plastic-lined cap, and label the bottle.

Making herb oil
Follow the above method, but instead of vinegar fill up the jar with virgin olive oil, sunflower oil, or grapeseed oil. Let infuse in a cool, dark place or the refrigerator. When the flavors have developed, strain and bottle.

Making herb or spice butter

Most fresh herbs make fine flavored butters; among spices, choose ground cumin, black pepper, cardamom, allspice, paprika, or cayenne – 1½–2 tbsp per ⅔ cup (150g) butter. If you combine spices with herbs, use less. Butters keep for a week if refrigerated, or can be frozen.

1 Beat ⅔ cup (150g) softened butter in a bowl with 1–2 tbsp lemon juice and 4–5 tbsp chopped herbs, or blend the butter and lemon juice with the same quantity of herbs in a food processor.

2 Lay a sheet of plastic wrap on a flat surface and spoon the flavored butter into the center. Press the butter into an elongated shape. Wrap in another sheet of plastic wrap to prevent tearing.

3 Taking care to avoid folding the wrap into the butter, roll the butter into a sausage shape. Twist the ends of the plastic wrap to compress the butter, wrap in foil, and refrigerate.

spices

I have long had a passion for spices and a fascination with their origins and production, as well as their culinary possibilities. What people eat in any particular region is, or was, largely determined by what grew and was reared there. The style of cooking originally depended on local conditions, such as the availability of fuels, but what really differentiates the great cuisines of the world is the spices they use and how they blend them.

Produce of tropical Asia

Most of the important spice plants – cinnamon, cloves, galangal, ginger, nutmeg, pepper – are native to the Asian tropics. They have been used and traded for millennia, and much has been written about the history of their trade – the fortunes and empires founded on it, the brutal conquests, piracy, and greed; but our view of these developments has always been a Western one.

We know about the overland routes from China to Byzantium, we are aware of the role Arab seafarers played in the introduction of spices to the Tigris-Euphrates basin and later to the Mediterranean ports, and we have read about the Portuguese, Dutch, and English monopolies. But we know little about the equally important early Asian trade, dominated at different times by the large merchant fleets first of the Korean kingdom of Silla (early 7th to mid-9th centuries), then of southern China under the Sung dynasty (960–1276), and of Sri Lanka. We know even less of the much earlier Indian traders who, from 600 BC, established new Hindu or Buddhist states in Sri Lanka, Malaysia, and some of the Indonesian islands, and supplied them with spices from their homeland.

When Columbus "discovered" America, the cultures of the continent were already old and highly developed, and the spices of the American tropics and subtropics – allspice, chili peppers, vanilla – had played their part in those cultures for a very long time.

Here Europeans can indeed be said to have been of importance, for the rapid spread of chilies throughout their colonies transformed the diet of half the world.

The spread of spices

Europe itself had already contributed much to the world of spices. Many of the aromatic seeds – coriander, fennel, fenugreek, mustard, poppy – are native to the Mediterranean region, and Europe's colder regions have contributed caraway, dill, and juniper. European trade remained mainly within the continent and with western Asia, but settlers sailing to the New World took many of their familiar spices with them.

Not all the spread of spices was due to trade. Some resulted from the breaking of jealously guarded monopolies; botanists and explorers smuggled plants to new destinations and plantations were established.

Migration has had a more lasting effect than trade on the spread of spices. For example, ships from southern China carried ginger, planted in troughs, as a necessity

CARDAMOM   POPPY   LEMON GRASS   GINGER

VANILLA
Cured vanilla beans, containing tiny, sticky seeds, flavor ice cream, cakes, and sweet syrups. Vanilla also goes well with seafood and chicken.

TURMERIC
Grated turmeric rhizome imparts a warm, earthy flavor to many Indian and Caribbean dishes, as well as giving them their rich yellow color.

TAMARIND
Tamarind is used to give a fruity acidity to many Asian dishes and preserves. Tamarind pulp is soaked in water before use.

of life, and so it came to be cultivated throughout the Pacific region. Immigrant communities, whether established by colonial force or economic plight, brought their own traditional ingredients and married them to local produce – hence Cape Malay and Cajun cooking, the "rijsttafel" of Holland, and the use of Colombo powder in the French West Indies.

The desire for authenticity

Today there is a growing awareness of and demand for authentic regional foods. Many ethnic restaurants define clearly their style of cooking: Cantonese, Sichuan, Hunan or Mughal cooking from the north of India and Keralan from the south. In our cities we can find the food of most countries in the world. What determines their individuality has much to do with how they use herbs and spices.

It has been said that chemistry is like cooking, but now it would be more accurate to say that cooking is becoming like chemistry. Food companies are constantly formulating new flavors and trying to synthesize others. They use electronic noses and tongues and other sophisticated apparatus to produce "aroma-fingerprints." They "collect headspace"

– that is, gather aroma molecules from spices, herbs, and fruits or from finished dishes for reproduction in a laboratory, eventually to be unleashed in ready-prepared foods. The results are certainly impressive, but many of the cultural, tactile, and nutritive values of the original foods are lost. Successfully making your own blend of spices gives a sense of achievement that nothing squeezed out of a tube or poured from a bottle can equal.

Choosing and using spices

Complex flavors are built up in mixtures by using spices (or herbs) that complement each other. Some are used for their taste, others for their aroma. Some have souring properties; in others, the color is important. The moment at which spices are added to a dish makes a crucial difference. Whether or not they are dry-roasted beforehand, they will impart their flavor to the dish if added at the beginning of cooking; if sprinkled on toward the end of cooking, it is their aroma that will be emphasized in the finished dish.

GRATING GINGER
Fresh ginger rhizome yields a highly aromatic juice. After fine grating, the ginger shavings are wrapped in cloth and the juice squeezed out.

GRINDING SPICES
Spices are best stored whole and ground only when needed. Many spices start to lose their aroma within hours of grinding.

FRYING SPICES
For some dishes the spices are fried in oil beforehand to impart their flavor. The oil is then used to flavor the dish.

NIGELLA
Nigella sativa

Nigella is the botanical name of love-in-a-mist, the pretty garden plant with pale blue flowers and feathery foliage. The species grown for its seed is a close but less decorative relative, native to western Asia and southern Europe, where it grows wild and in cultivation. India is the largest producer of nigella and a large consumer. The small, black seeds are often misnamed and sold as black onion seed.

Culinary uses

Nigella is sprinkled on flatbreads, rolls, and savory pastries, alone or with sesame or cumin. Cooks in Bengal combine it with mustard seeds, cumin, fennel, and fenugreek in the local spice mixture, panch phoron, which gives a distinctive taste to legume and vegetable dishes. Elsewhere in India, nigella is used in pilafs, kormas, and curries, and in pickles. In Iran, it is a popular pickling spice used for fruit and vegetables. It is good with roast potatoes and other root vegetables. Ground with coriander and cumin, it adds depth to a Middle-Eastern potato or mixed vegetable omelette.
Essential to panch phoron.
Good with breads, legumes, rice, green and root vegetables.
Combines well with allspice, cardamom, cinnamon, coriander, cumin, fennel, ginger, pepper, savory, thyme, turmeric.

Whole seeds

Indian cooks usually dry-roast or fry the seeds to develop their flavor before sprinkling them over vegetarian dishes and salads.

SESAME

Sesamum orientale

Sesame is one of the earliest recorded plants grown for its seeds. The Egyptians and Babylonians used ground seeds in their breads, a practice that continues in the Middle East today. Excavations in eastern Turkey have found evidence of oil being extracted from the seeds as early as 900BC. High in polyunsaturated fatty acids, the oil pressed from raw seeds is excellent for cooking and is highly stable, with the advantage that it does not turn rancid in hot climates.

TASTING NOTES

Sesame seeds are not very aromatic but they have a mildly nutty, earthy odor. This is more marked in the taste, which develops even greater richness after dry-roasting or grinding to a paste. Black seeds have an earthier taste than white and are not usually ground.

PARTS USED

Seeds, whole and as a paste, and oil.

BUYING AND STORING

Sesame seeds are available from supermarkets and Middle Eastern and wholefood stores, as are the pale brown sesame paste (tahini), darker Chinese sesame paste and sesame oils (light and nutty sesame oil and darker, stronger Asian sesame oil). Golden seeds, with their richer aroma, are preferred by Japanese cooks, but these are harder to find. Store seeds in airtight containers and toast them as needed.

HARVESTING

Plants are harvested before the seed pods are fully ripe, when they burst open. The pods are dried and hulled, usually mechanically.

Whole seeds

Produced by an annual tropical plant, sesame seeds may be pale gold or white, red, brown, or black, depending on the variety. The seeds are small, flat, and oval, shiny and waxy because of their oil content, and fairly soft. The creamy white seeds are the most common.

Culinary uses

Sesame is scattered over breads or ground and added to the dough before baking. It is essential to the Middle Eastern spice blend za'atar, and to Japanese seven-spice powder. It is the main ingredient of the Middle Eastern sweetmeat, halva. In India, sesame is used in sweets such as til laddoos, which are balls of sesame and jaggery flavored with cardamom. Indian cooks use pale golden sesame oil, called gingili or til oil, for cooking. Tahini and the oil are made from raw seeds.

Deep brown Chinese sesame paste and amber-colored Asian oil are made from dry-roasted seeds; this enhances the nutty flavor and gives the darker color. These products are used in Chinese, Korean, and Japanese cooking. Asian oil is a seasoning oil, not a cooking oil, because it burns at low temperatures. Chinese sesame paste has a dense texture and is used in dressings for noodles, rice, and vegetables.

The Chinese like the crunchy texture of sesame seeds to coat shrimp balls and shrimp toasts. In Japan, white or golden sesame is blended with soy sauce and sugar to dress cold chicken, noodles, and vegetable salads.

Black sesame is used in Chinese and Japanese cooking as a garnish for rice and vegetables, and to coat fish and seafood before cooking. It is often said to be bitter if dry-roasted, but I have not found it so if done lightly, and Japanese cooks frequently use it dry-roasted. Blended with coarse salt it makes the Japanese condiment, goma shio, which is sprinkled over vegetables, salads, and rice. In China, black seeds coat deep-fried toffee apples and bananas.

Essential to za'atar, goma shio, seven-spice powder.

Good with eggplant, fish, green vegetables, honey, legumes, lemon, noodles, rice, salad greens, sugar, zucchini.

Combines well with cardamom, cassia, chili, cinnamon, cloves, coriander, ginger, nutmeg, oregano, pepper, sumac, thyme.

ASIAN SESAME OIL
Asian oil is usually added to dishes before serving. Combined with chili, garlic, and ginger, it is popular in Sichuan cooking.

TAHINI
In the Middle East, pale brown tahini is blended with garlic and lemon juice to make a paste, used as a basis for dressings for vegetable and fish dishes, and as the flavoring for the chickpea dip, hummus.

POPPY
Papaver somniferum

The aroma of dark seeds is lightly nutty and sweet; the flavor is stronger and somewhat almond-like. White seeds are lighter and more mellow in flavor. Both the aroma and flavor are enhanced by dry-roasting or baking. Poppy seeds are rich in protein and oil.

PARTS USED

Seeds.

BUYING AND STORING

Poppy seeds may be slate-blue, creamy-white, or mid-brown. The latter are common in Turkey and the Middle East; the blue-gray seeds are most used in Europe, and the creamy-white seeds in India. Blue poppy seeds are available from supermarkets; the white and brown can be bought from spice merchants or in Asian and Middle Eastern markets. The seeds tend to go rancid quickly because of their high oil content, so buy in small amounts and use quickly. Store in an airtight container, or in the freezer if you intend to keep them longer than a few months.

HARVESTING

Plants are harvested mechanically when the seedheads turn yellow-brown; the capsules are cut off and dried.

The opium poppy – *Papaver somniferum* means "sleep-inducing poppy" – is a plant of great antiquity, native from the eastern Mediterranean to central Asia. It has been cultivated since earliest times for opium, a narcotic latex that oozes from unripe seedpods if they are cut, and for its ripe seeds. Neither the seeds nor the dried pods from which they are harvested have narcotic properties.

Culinary uses

In the West, poppy seeds are sprinkled over or incorporated into breads, bagels, pretzels, and cakes. Ground to a paste with honey or sugar, they are used to fill strudels and other pastries. In Turkey, roasted, ground seeds are made into halva or desserts with syrup and nuts. In India, the roasted seeds are ground and combined with spices to flavor and thicken kormas, curries, and gravies. They are used extensively in Bengali cooking in shuktas (bitter vegetable stews) and to coat crusty, dry-textured vegetables. Use poppy seeds, with or without other spices, in dressings for noodles or to garnish vegetables.
Good with eggplant, green beans, breads and pastries, cauliflower, potatoes, zucchini.

Whole seeds

Poppy seeds do not grind easily, but dry-roasting followed by a blitz in a spice mill or coffee grinder can help. If they are to be used to thicken a dish, cover them with a little water and soak for several hours, then process them briefly together with the liquid.

ROSE
Rosa species

Throughout the Arab world, Turkey, and Iran, and as far east as northern India, dried rosebuds or petals and rose water are consumed in a variety of ways. Turkey and Bulgaria are the biggest producers of attar of roses (the essential oil), but roses are also grown commercially in Iran and Morocco. Most of the flowers are processed to make rose water, but you can also buy the wonderfully scented, dried pink buds.

Culinary uses

In Bengal and Punjab, rose water features prominently in desserts such as gulab jamun (*gulab* means rose) and kheer (a rich rice pudding). Its flavor can also be detected in much Turkish delight, in Middle Eastern pastries, and in some savory dishes. Fresh or dried petals are infused in syrups to make desserts and drinks. Iranian and Tunisian cooks use rosebuds in spice blends for rice and stews; in Morocco rose water is used more than rosebuds.

Essential to Iranian advieh, ras el hanout, Tunisian bharat.
Good with apples, apricots, chestnuts, lamb, poultry, quinces, rice, desserts and pastries.
Combines well with cardamom, chili, cinnamon, cloves, coriander, cumin, pepper, saffron, turmeric, yogurt.

CINNAMON

Cinnamomum zelanicum

True cinnamon is indigenous to Sri Lanka. Like cassia, it is the bark of an evergreen tree of the laurel family. For 200 years a highly profitable monopoly of the island's cinnamon was controlled first by the Portuguese, then the Dutch, and finally by the English. By the late 18th century, cinnamon had been planted in Java, India, and the Seychelles, and the monopoly could no longer be sustained.

TASTING NOTES

Cinnamon has a warm, agreeably sweet, woody aroma that is delicate yet intense; the taste is fragrant and warm with hints of clove and citrus. The presence of eugenol in the essential oil distinguishes cinnamon from cassia, giving it the note of clove.

PARTS USED

Quills of dried bark, ground cinnamon.

BUYING AND STORING

Ground cinnamon – the paler its color, the finer its quality – is widely available, but it loses its flavor quite quickly, so buy in small amounts. Whole quills are available from specialty spice merchants and some supermarkets. They keep their aroma for 2–3 years if stored in an airtight container.

HARVESTING

The Sri Lankan cinnamon gardens lie on the coastal plains south of Colombo. Seedlings grow in thick clumps, with shoots about the thickness of a thumb. In the rainy season the shoots are cut off at the base and peeled. The harvesters work with extraordinary dexterity to cut the paper-thin pieces of bark and then roll quills over 3ft (up to 1m) long by hand. The quills are then gently dried in the shade.

Quills
Pale brown or tan strips of dried bark are rolled one into another to form long, slender, smooth quills.

GRADES OF CINNAMON
There are many grades of cinnamon; quills are classified as Continental, Mexican, or Hamburg, according to their thickness; the thin Continental quills have the finest flavor. Quillings are quills broken in handling; featherings are the small inner pieces of bark not large enough to use in quills; and chips are shavings, the lowest grade of cinnamon. Featherings and chips are mostly used to produce ground cinnamon.

Culinary uses

Cinnamon's subtle flavor is well suited to all manner of desserts and spiced breads and cakes; it combines particularly well with chocolate and with apples, bananas, and pears. Use it in apple pie or with baked apples, with bananas fried in butter and flavored with rum, and in red wine used for poaching pears. It also makes an excellent flavoring for many meat and vegetable dishes in Middle Eastern and Indian cuisine. Moroccan cooks use it widely in lamb or chicken tagines, in the stew to accompany couscous, and above all to flavor bstilla, a pie of crisp, layered pastry filled with squab and almonds. The glorious Arab stew of lamb with apricots – mishmisheya – uses cinnamon and other spices, and it plays a role in many an Iranian khoresh (stews that accompany rice). In India, cinnamon is used in many masalas (spice mixtures), in chutneys and condiments, and in spiced pilafs.

Mexico is the main importer of cinnamon, which is used to flavor coffee and chocolate drinks; cinnamon tea is popular throughout Central and South America. Once popular for spicing ale, cinnamon, together with cloves, sugar, and sliced oranges, makes an excellent flavoring for mulled wine.

Good with almonds, apples, apricots, bananas, chocolate, coffee, eggplant, lamb, pears, poultry, rice.

Combines well with cardamom, cloves, coriander, cumin, ginger, mace, mastic, nutmeg, tamarind, turmeric.

GROUND BARK
Ground cinnamon is immediately aromatic; quills tend to hide their aromatic properties until broken or cooked in a liquid.

CASSIA
Cinnamomum cassia

Cassia is the dried bark of a species of laurel tree native to Assam and northern Burma. It is recorded in a Chinese herbal in 2700BC, and today most cassia is exported from southern China and Vietnam. The finest quality comes from northern Vietnam. Cassia and cinnamon are used interchangeably in many countries. In the US, cassia is sold as cinnamon or cassia-cinnamon, and is preferred to true cinnamon because of its more pronounced aroma and flavor.

PARTS USED

Dried bark and quills, ground bark; dried unripe fruits, called cassia buds; tejpat leaves.

BUYING AND STORING

Cassia is difficult to grind, so it may be better to buy a small amount of ground cassia as well as pieces or quills. The latter will keep their flavor much longer, up to 2 years if stored in an airtight container. Buy bark, buds, and leaves from specialist spice dealers and keep in an airtight container.

HARVESTING

Harvesting starts in the rainy season when the bark can be stripped easily. As it dries it curls to make quills, which are graded according to their essential oil content, length, and color. Quills are reddish-brown and the layers are thicker than in cinnamon quills. Cassia bark is thicker and coarser than cinnamon, and the corky outer layer is often left on when it is sold in pieces.

Whole bark
The color of the smooth inner bark is reddish-brown, the rough outside is gray-brown.

QUILLS
Cassia bark is thick and tough and its quills are simple, crude curls, whereas the thinner, softer bark of cinnamon is rolled more tightly.

Buds

Cassia buds are a bit like small cloves. The hard, red-brown seed is just visible in the wrinkled gray-brown calyx. The buds have a warm, mellow aroma and the flavor is musky, sweet, and pungent, but less concentrated than that of the bark.

Dried tejpat leaves

Leaves of the related *C. tamala* are oval in shape with three long veins. They are used in the cooking of north India. Dried tejpat leaves have an immediate smell of spiced tea. A prolonged sniff reveals a warm, musky aroma of clove and cinnamon with citrus undertones.

Culinary uses

Cassia is an essential spice in China, where it is frequently used whole to flavor braised dishes and sauces for cooking meat and poultry; and ground cassia is a constituent of five-spice powder. In India, it is found in curries and pilafs, and in Germany and Russia, it is often used as a flavoring for chocolate. I prefer cinnamon to cassia for delicate desserts, but it is good with apples, plums, dried figs, and prunes.

Cassia is used in spice blends for baking and sweet dishes. The pungency of cassia is better suited than cinnamon to rich meats such as duck or pork, and it goes well with pumpkin and other winter squashes, with sweet potatoes, and with lentils and beans. Cassia buds are used in sweet pickles in the Asia, and they can be used, whole, in place of cassia. They are particularly good in fruit compotes.

Tejpat leaves are often called Indian bay leaves, because both come from species of laurel and because they are both used in long-cooked dishes and removed before serving. However, tejpat leaves are quite different from bay aromatically and a clove or a small piece of cassia make a better substitute than bay if you can't find tejpat leaves. The leaves are used extensively in the biryanis and kormas of northern India and in some garam masalas.

Indonesian or Korintje cassia, *C. burmannii,* from Sumatra has a deep color and a pleasantly spicy flavor, but lacks the depth of Vietnamese or Chinese cassia.

Essential to five-spice powder.

Good with apples, plums, prunes, legumes, meat and poultry, root vegetables.

Combines well with cardamom, cloves, coriander, cumin, fennel, ginger, mace, nutmeg, Sichuan pepper, star anise, turmeric.

CORIANDER
Coriandrum sativum

A few plants serve cooks as both herb and spice, and of these coriander is undoubtedly the most widely used in both its forms. As a spice crop it is grown in eastern Europe, India, the US, and Central America, as well as in its native habitat of western Asia and the Mediterranean. In all of these regions it is used extensively, sometimes in combination with its leaf, commonly called cilantro.

Whole Moroccan seeds
Spherical Moroccan seeds are more commonly available than the oval Indian variety.

GROUND SEEDS
Seeds are brittle and easy to grind; dry-roasting before grinding enhances the flavor.

Culinary uses

Cooks use coriander seeds in larger amounts than they do many other spices because the flavor is mild. After dry-roasting, coriander forms the basis of many curry powders and masalas. North African cooks use it in harissa, tabil, ras el hanout, and other spice mixtures. Georgian khmeli-suneli and Iranian advieh mixtures usually include it, as do Middle Eastern baharat blends; throughout the region coriander is a popular flavoring for vegetable dishes, stews, and sausages. Crushed green olives that are flavored with coriander are a specialty of Cyprus. In Europe and the US, coriander serves as a pickling spice and gives a pleasant, mild flavor to sweet-sour pickles and chutneys. West Indian cooks use it in masalas, and in Mexico it is often paired with cumin. French vegetable dishes à la grecque are flavored with coriander. It is a useful spice to add to marinades, to court-bouillon for fish, or to stock for soup. It is also a constituent of English mixed sweet spice, much used in cakes and cookies. Its flavor combines well with those of autumn fruits – apples, plums, pears, quinces – baked in pies or stewed in compotes.

Essential to harissa, tabil, dukka, most masalas.

Good with apples, chicken, citrus fruit, fish, ham, mushrooms, onions, plums, pork, potatoes.

Combines well with allspice, chili, cinnamon, cloves, cumin, fennel, garlic, ginger, mace, nutmeg.

Whole Indian seeds

Although coriander seeds and leaves smell and taste quite different, they complement each other in Indian and Mexican dishes.

GROUND SEEDS
Indian coriander has a sweeter flavor than Moroccan.

JUNIPER

Juniperus communis

The aroma of juniper is pleasantly woody, bittersweet, and unmistakably like gin. The taste is clean and refreshing, sweetish with a slight burning effect, and has a hint of pine and resin.

Juniper is a prickly, evergreen shrub or small tree that grows throughout much of the northern hemisphere, especially on chalky, hilly sites. It is a member of the large cypress family, the only one with edible fruit. The berries were used by enterprising Romans to adulterate pepper, and were burned in the Middle Ages (and well beyond) to clean the air of pestilence. Juniper's use as a flavoring for gin and other spirits dates back at least to the 17th century.

PARTS USED

Berries, fresh or dried.

BUYING AND STORING

Juniper berries are always sold whole and are usually dried. They are quite soft and bruise easily, so make sure those you buy are whole and dry. They will keep for several months in an airtight jar.

Whole berries
Berries growing in southerly latitudes have more flavor. If you come across them in the wild, ripe and blue-black, it is well worth picking them.

HARVESTING

A juniper bush makes a handsome garden plant all year round. The purple-black, smooth berries are about the size of a small pea. They take 2–3 years to ripen, so green and ripe berries occur on the same plant. There is some cultivation of juniper and also berries are gathered in the wild – a hazardous undertaking because of the very sharp, spiky leaves. Berries are picked when ripe, in autumn. Freshly picked berries have a green-blue bloom that disappears during drying.

Culinary uses

Juniper is perhaps best known as the flavoring for gin as well as for other spirits and cordials, but the berries also have many culinary uses. Juniper is a natural foil for game and for fatty foods. The Scandinavians add it to marinades for pickled beef and elk and to red-wine marinades for roast pork. In northern France, juniper appears in venison dishes and pâtés; in Belgium, it is used with veal kidneys flamed in gin; and in Alsace and Germany, it is a flavoring for sauerkraut.

Easily crushed in a mortar, the berries impart a mild but pungent flavor that can benefit many dishes, both savory and sweet. Mixed with salt and garlic they can be rubbed onto lamb, pork, game birds, and venison. Another dry-salting mixture that relies on juniper is that for Elizabeth David's spiced beef.

Crushed berries also go into brines and marinades; chopped finely, just a few liven up stuffings and pâtés and make good sauces for hearty meats. Crush or grind juniper just before using it: in contact with the air the essential oils are quickly lost.

Good with apples, beef, cabbage, duck, game, goose, pork.

Combines well with bay, caraway, celery, garlic, marjoram, pepper, rosemary, savory, thyme.

A rub for meats

Juniper berries crushed in a mortar with garlic and coarse salt make a well-flavored rub for lamb, pork, and venison.

VANILLA
Vanilla planifolia

TASTING NOTES

Fresh vanilla beans have no aroma or taste. After fermentation they develop a rich, mellow, intensely perfumed aroma with hints of licorice or tobacco matched by a delicate, sweetly fruity or creamy flavor. There may also be hints of raisin or prune, or smoky, spicy notes.

PARTS USED

Cured pods (beans).

BUYING AND STORING

You are more likely to get better grade beans from a specialty food store or mail order than a supermarket. Stored away from the light in an airtight container, vanilla beans will keep for 2 years or more. When buying extract, look for bottles labeled "pure vanilla extract," which by law must contain 35 percent alcohol by volume.

HARVESTING

Vanilla pods are picked when they begin to turn yellow. Further maturation is prevented by plunging them into boiling water, then they are sun-dried by day and sweated by night, wrapped in blankets. The pods shrivel and darken, and enzymes cause a chemical change that produces aromatic compounds, notably vanillin. About 11lb (5kg) of fresh pods yields 2¼lb (1kg) cured vanilla beans.

Vanilla is the fruit of a perennial, climbing orchid, native to Central America. It is not known when vanilla was first cured and used as a flavoring, but tribes ruled by the Aztecs had fairly sophisticated methods of fermenting the bean-like fruits to extract vanillin crystals. The Spanish conquistadors drank chocolate flavored with vanilla at the court of Moctezuma. They took to it and shipped both chocolate and vanilla back to Spain. They also gave the fruit its name: vanilla is the diminutive of *vaina*, meaning pod. Today, vanilla is exported from Mexico, Réunion, Madagascar, Tahiti, and Indonesia.

Whole dried beans
Good vanilla beans are deep brown or black, long and narrow, somewhat wrinkled, moist, waxy, supple, and immediately fragrant.

SEEDS
The tiny, sticky, black seeds can be scraped from the bean with the point of a knife.

Culinary uses

In India and Southeast Asia, tamarind is used as an acidulant (much as the West uses lemon and lime) in curries, sambhars, chutneys, marinades, preserves, pickles, and sherbets. Tamarind gives many hot south Indian dishes, such as Goan vindaloo and Gujarati vegetable stews, their characteristic sourness. With raw sugar and chili peppers, it is simmered to a syrupy dipping sauce for fish. It goes into Thai tom yom soup and Chinese hot-and-sour ones. In Indonesia, where the word *asem* means both tamarind and sour, it is used in sauces, both savory and sweet, and for marinades. On Java, it is preferred to lemon for the island's sweet-sour dishes. In India, ground seeds are used in cakes. In Iran, stuffed vegetables are baked in a rich tamarind stock. In the Middle East, a lemonade-like drink made from tamarind syrup is popular; Central America and the West Indies also have tamarind drinks, which are consumed on their own or in tropical fruit punch, or made into milk shakes with ice cream. Jamaica uses tamarind in stews and with rice; in Costa Rica it makes a sour sauce. In Thailand, Vietnam, the Philippines, Jamaica, and Cuba, tamarind pulp is eaten as a sweetmeat, dusted with sugar or candied. Try using tamarind with salt as a rub for fish or meat before cooking, or with soy sauce and ginger in a marinade for pork or lamb.

Essential to Worcestershire sauce.

Good with cabbage, chicken, fish and shellfish, lamb, lentils, mushrooms, peanuts, pork, poultry, most vegetables.

Combines well with asafetida, chili, cilantro, cumin, galangal, garlic, ginger, mustard, shrimp paste (blachan, trassi), soy sauce, (brown or palm) sugar, turmeric.

BLOCK
To use tamarind from a block, soak a small piece, about the equivalent of 1 tbsp, for 10–15 minutes in a little hot water. Stir to loosen the pulp, squeeze out, and strain to remove fiber and, if they are present, seeds.

CONCENTRATE OR SYRUP
Tamarind concentrate has a "cooked" smell reminiscent of molasses, and a distinct sharp, acid taste. To use a concentrate, stir 1–2 tsp into a little water.

PASTE
Adding prepared tamarind to dishes moderates the heating effect of fiery chili peppers and hot spices.

acidic and fruity spices

SUMAC

Rhus coriaria

Sumac is only slightly aromatic; the taste is pleasantly tart, fruity, and astringent.

Sumac is the fruit of a decorative, bushy shrub that grows to a height of about 10ft (3m) and has light gray or reddish stems. The shrub grows wild on sparsely wooded uplands and high plateaux around the Mediterranean, especially in Sicily, where it is widely cultivated. Sumac also grows in parts of the Middle East, notably in Turkey (Anatolia) and in its native Iran.

Culinary uses

Sumac is an essential ingredient in Arab and, especially, in Lebanese cooking, where it is used as an acidulant. Its taste is tingling and tart and it brings out the flavours of food to which is added, much as salt does. If the berries are used whole they are cracked and soaked in water for 20–30 minutes, then squeezed out well to extract all the juice, which is used for marinades and salad dressings, in meat and vegetable dishes, and also to make a refreshing drink. Sumac powder is rubbed onto food before cooking: the Lebanese and Syrians use it on fish, the Iranians and Georgians on kebabs, the Iraqis and Turks on vegetables. Sumac is often sprinkled on flatbreads; it provides the tart element in the Lebanese bread salad, fattoush, and is an essential part of the spice and herb blend za'atar.

PARTS USED

Dried berries.

BUYING AND STORING

Outside the growing regions sumac is normally only available as a coarse or fine powder. In an airtight container this will keep for several months. Whole berries can be kept for a year or more.

HARVESTING

In the autumn sumac leaves turn a beautiful red, and the white flowers eventually develop into dense, conical clusters of fruit – small, round, russet-colored berries. The berries are picked just before they are fully ripe, dried in the sun, and crushed to a brick-red or red-brown powder.

GROUND BERRIES
Berries vary in color from brick red to red-brown or maroon, depending on where they come from.

BARBERRY
Berberis vulgaris

TASTING NOTES

The ripe berries are pleasantly acidulous. Dried berries have a light aroma, reminiscent of currants, but with a tart note. The taste is agreeably sweet-tart, with an underlying sharpness that derives from malic acid.

PARTS USED

Berries, fresh and dried.

BUYING AND STORING

Dried barberries are difficult to buy outside their region of production, except from Iranian markets. Plants can be found in nurseries and make attractive ornamental shrubs. If you grow one, or have found a bush in the wild, you can easily gather your own berries (provided you wear gloves to do so) and dry them. Dried berries will keep for several months. They retain their color and flavor best if stored in the freezer.

HARVESTING

The small, oblong berries hang down in tight clusters and can be picked from July until late summer. In Iran, the Caucasian republics, and countries further east, barberries are still gathered from the wild, sun-dried, and stored for use in the kitchen.

Many species of the *Berberis* genus and of the closely related genus *Mahonia* grow wild in temperate zones of Europe, Asia, northern Africa, and North America. They are dense, spiny, perennial bushes with toothed leaves, and they all have edible berries – the *Berberis* berries some shade of red, the *Mahonia* ones blue. Barberries are used as a spice in central Asia and the Caucasus region. In New England, ripe barberries are used in pies, preserves and syrups; green (unripe) barberries are sometimes pickled.

Culinary uses

Barberries are usually preserved in syrup or vinegar to make a tart flavoring. Being rich in pectin they are easily made into preserves. In central Asia and in Iran, dried berries are used to add a sour flavor and a splash of color to pilafs; they also go into stuffings, stews, and meat dishes.

Dried berries soon release their flavor if fried gently in butter or oil. They are sprinkled over some rice dishes. In Georgia, I was given a mixture of crushed barberries and salt – this is rubbed on lamb kebabs before grilling, giving the meat a tart piquancy. In India, dried berries are added to desserts, rather like sour currants. Fresh berries strewn over lamb or mutton for the last minutes of roasting will burst and coat the meat with their tart juice.

POMEGRANATE

Punica granatum

The pomegranate is a small, deciduous tree with narrow, leathery leaves, brilliant orange-red flowers, and large, beige to red-skinned fruits. Native from Iran to the Himalayas, it has been cultivated since ancient times all around the Mediterranean basin. Pomegranates now grow throughout the drier parts of subtropical India and Southeast Asia, Indonesia, and China, as well as in tropical Africa. The trees are very long-lived, but their vigor declines after only 15–20 years.

TASTING NOTES

The seeds are fleshy and taste both sweet and acidic. Middle Eastern pomegranates tend to be sweeter than those grown in India, which can have a slightly bitter aftertaste. The juice varies in color from a light pink to a deep red; it is sweet but with a refreshing sharpness.

PARTS USED

The seeds are used fresh and dried.

BUYING AND STORING

Pomegranates will keep for weeks in a cool place, and storing improves both flavor and juice content. Once extracted, the seeds or the juice can be frozen. Pomegranate molasses is a dark, thick, sticky syrup, stocked in Iranian and Middle Eastern markets and in some supermarkets. Anardana (dried berries) can be found in Indian markets, either whole, when they should be a deep, dark red, or ground. Anardana and molasses keep well.

HARVESTING

The fruit ripens in October and must be picked before it splits open to release the seeds. In northern India, the seeds of the sour and bitterish wild pomegranate are sun-dried for 2 weeks to make anardana.

Whole fruit
Choose fruit with the deepest color you can find. The seeds are really transparent juice sacs holding pulp and one (usually very hard) seed.

ANARDANA (DRIED SEEDS)
Dried seeds are pleasantly
tart to smell and have a
sweet-sour taste.

MOLASSES
Pomegranate molasses may be
sweet or sweet-sour, the fruity
sweetness tempered by an
attractive tartness. The flavor is
more concentrated than that of
grenadine syrup.

Culinary uses

In the Middle East and central Asia,
fresh, whole seeds are sprinkled over
salads and pastes like hummus or
tahina, or as a garnish on desserts.
They are very good with chicken,
can be added to stews, and will liven
up a fruit or cucumber salad.

The seeds can be pressed, and
the juice of the sweeter varieties is
a popular beverage in the Middle
East; in Georgia, tart juice is widely
used in sauces for meat and fish.

Pomegranate molasses, a thick,
dark syrup, is also made from the
juice. Molasses can be brushed
onto chicken or meat to act as a
marinade, or added to slow-cooked
dishes. Its taste and degree of
sourness vary greatly from region
to region. Arab and Indian molasses
tends to be quite tart, even sour.
Iran produces a sweeter version,
which is an essential ingredient of
muhammarah, a Middle-Eastern
dip made with hot chili peppers and
walnuts, and of fesenjan, a richly
flavored Iranian duck or chicken
dish made with walnuts. There is
also a good Iranian winter soup
based on pomegranate molasses.

Anardana (dried berries), which
look like red-black raisins, are
sticky but have a hard crunch. Their
fruity, tangy flavor is much liked in
northern India. They go into curries
and chutneys, into stuffings for
bread and savory pastries, and into
braised vegetable dishes. In Punjabi
cooking they flavor legumes. They
give the food a more subtle sweet-
sour taste than amchoor would,
and are either soaked in water like
tamarind, or crushed and sprinkled
directly onto food.

Good with avocado, beets,
cucumber, fish, lamb, legumes, pine
nuts, poultry, spinach, walnuts.
Combines well with allspice,
cardamom, chili, cinnamon, cloves,
coriander, cumin, fenugreek, ginger,
golpar, rosebuds, turmeric.

KOKAM

Garcinia indica

Kokam is the fruit of a slender, graceful tree native to the tropical rainforests along the thin ribbon of the Malabar (Malwani) coast of India from Mumbai to Cochin. In its native region, which includes Maharashtra, Karnataka, and Kerala, it is used as an acidulant, much as tamarind is in other parts of India. Fairly recently it has become popular in the US, the Middle East, and Australia, but it still has to make its mark in Europe.

PARTS USED

Whole fruit or rind.

BUYING AND STORING

Dried rind can be bought from Indian markets and spice merchants; they may also have kokam paste. In an airtight jar both will keep for up to a year. The deeper the skin color, the better the kokam. Kokam is often labeled black mangosteen.

HARVESTING

Kokam is a smallish, round, sticky fruit, the size of a plum but with an uneven surface. It is dark purple when ripe and ready for picking, in April or May. The fruit is dried whole or split -- which leaves the pulp full of the half dozen or more fairly big seeds. Alternatively, the rind is removed, soaked in the liquid of the pulp, and then dried in the sun. Its local name is *amsul*, literally sour rind. The dried rind comes folded into small strips that have a leathery appearance.

Culinary uses

Kokam is used as a souring agent, milder than tamarind. Dried fruit or rind are usually soaked in water; the pulp softens and is pressed dry, and the liquid is used for cooking beans or vegetables. Kokam rinds are often rubbed with salt to speed the drying; when using them, check that the dish does not become too salty.

Kokam saar – made by boiling pieces of kokam in water, straining the liquid, and flavoring it with different combinations of fresh ginger, onion, chili peppers, cumin, or coriander – is served both as an appetizer and as a cooling accompaniment to fiery, coconut-based fish curries. In Kerala, kokam is known as "fish tamarind."

With coconut milk, and with or without jaggery, kokam makes sol kadhi, a fragrant, carmine-colored beverage. **Good with** beans, eggplant, fish and shellfish, lentils, okra, plantain, potatoes, squash.

Combines well with cardamom, chili, coconut milk, coriander, cumin, fenugreek, garlic, ginger, mustard seed, turmeric.

AMCHOOR
Mangifera indica

Amchoor is made from mangoes. The evergreen mango is native to India and Southeast Asia and is widely cultivated for its fruit. The trees crop every other year and continue to do so for well over a century. Every part of the tree is utilized in some way – bark, resin, leaves, flowers, seeds. The fruits are eaten fresh; both green (unripe) and ripe mangoes are made into chutneys and pickles. The spice is made from unripe fruit and is produced in India only.

Culinary uses

Amchoor is used as an acidulant in north Indian cooking in the way tamarind is used in the south. It gives a tang of tropical fruit to vegetable stews and soups, potato pakoras, and samosa fillings. It is good with stir-fried vegetables and in stuffings for breads and pastries. It is an essential ingredient in chat masala, a fresh-tasting and astringent spice blend from the Punjab, used for vegetable and legume dishes and for fruit salads. Amchoor is good in marinades to tenderize poultry, fish and meat, particularly meat to be grilled in a tandoor. It is also much used as a sourish flavoring in dals and chutneys.

AMCHOOR POWDER
This lumpy powder is easily crushed and provides acidity without adding moisture.

LEMON GRASS

Cymbopogon citratus

The flavor of lemon grass is refreshingly tart, clean, and citruslike with peppery notes. Freeze-dried lemon grass keeps its aroma quite well, but air-dried lemon grass loses its volatile oils; grated lemon rind gives more flavor than dried lemon grass.

PARTS USED

The lower part of the stalk, white and tinged with pale green.

BUYING AND STORING

Fresh lemon grass can be found in Asian markets and specialty produce markets. Buy firm stalks; they should not be wrinkled or dry. Fresh lemon grass will keep for 2–3 weeks in the refrigerator if wrapped in plastic. It also freezes well for up to 6 months. Freeze-dried lemon grass is quite fragrant and has a long shelf life in an airtight container. Dried lemon grass and lemon grass purée are available, but lack flavor.

HARVESTING

Most gardens in Singapore, Thailand, and Vietnam have a patch of lemon grass from which the cook can pluck a stalk or two. Commercial harvesting is done every 3–4 months. The leaves are removed before lemon grass is sold.

A showy, tropical grass with fibrous, sharp-edged leaves, lemon grass soon forms into large, dense clumps. It flourishes in temperate climates if it is overwintered indoors. The bulbous base imparts an elusive aromatic and lemon fragrance to the cooking of Southeast Asia. Previously hard to find outside that region, fresh lemon grass is now more widely available, thanks to the increased appreciation of Thai, Malay, Vietnamese, and Indonesian food. It is cultivated in Australia, Brazil, Mexico, West Africa, and in Florida and California.

Whole fresh stalks
Lemon grass contains citral, the flavor component of lemon rind. It gives the plant a subtle but sustained lemon fragrance.

Culinary uses

Remove the two outer layers and bruise the stalk if the lemon grass is to be used whole to flavor a stew or curry; take it out before serving. If the lemon grass is intended to be eaten as an ingredient of a soup or salad, discard the top part and slice the rest into very fine rings. Start at the bottom and stop slicing when the stalk becomes too hard – big pieces are unpleasantly fibrous to chew. Pounded with other spices and herbs, lemon grass goes into pastes to flavor curries, stews, and stir-fried dishes.

Lemon grass is a key ingredient in the Nonya cooking of Singapore and the southern part of the Malay peninsula. It is used in Thai larp, curries, and soups; in Vietnamese salads and spring rolls; in Indonesian bumbus (spice blends) for chicken and pork. Sri Lankan cooks use it in combination with coconut. Although it grows in India, it is not much used there except to make tea. If you grow the plant, the upper part of the leaves makes a pleasant, refreshing tea.

Lemon grass has a place in Western cooking, too. It suits all fish and seafood, especially crab and scallops. Add it to the stock for poaching fish or chicken. To flavor a vinaigrette, steep a few chopped stalks in it for 24 hours. Lemon grass is also good with fruit: use it, alone or with ginger or fennel seeds, to flavor syrups made for poaching peaches or pears.

Good with beef, chicken, fish and seafood, noodles, pork, variety meat, most vegetables.
Combines well with basil, chili, cilantro, cinnamon, cloves, coconut milk, galangal, garlic, ginger, turmeric.

FINELY SLICED STALK
Slices cut from fresh lemon grass often show purplish rings.

BRUISED STALKS
Bruising releases the volatile oils that impart flavor.

citrus spices

KAFFIR LIME
Citrus hystrix

TASTING NOTES

Leaves have an explosive fragrance, cleanly floral and citrus – not quite lemon, not quite lime. Their aroma and flavor are assertive and lingering, yet delicate. The rind of the fruit is slightly bitter with a strong citrus note. Dried leaves and dried rind lack the intense aroma of fresh.

Harvested from a shrubby, evergreen tree native to Southeast Asia, the rind and leaves of the kaffir lime have long imparted a clean, citrus flavor to the dishes of the region. Kaffir lime is now also grown in Florida, California, and Australia. The English name kaffir may originate in colonial usage or be a corruption of another word; some cooks may prefer to call this spice by its Thai name, makrut lime.

PARTS USED

Leaves and rind, preferably fresh.

BUYING AND STORING

Fresh leaves are available from Asian markets and some supermarkets. They keep for weeks in a plastic bag in the refrigerator. The leaves freeze well for up to a year, losing neither texture nor aromatics. Fruits should be firm and feel heavy for their size. Store in the refrigerator or in a cool room, as other citrus fruits. Dried leaves and rind are available; leaves should be green, not yellow or dingy-looking. Store both in airtight containers. Leaves will keep for 6–8 months. Some markets also stock rind preserved in brine.

HARVESTING

Leaves and fruit are picked and sold fresh or dried.

Whole fresh leaves
The leathery leaves grow in an unusual double form, as two on a single petiole. The upper side is dark green and glossy, the underside lighter and mat.

SHREDDED FRESH LEAVES
If the leaves are to be eaten, rather than removed before serving, break apart the pairs and remove the thick, central rib. Stack several leaves and shred finely.

Culinary uses

Lime leaves are responsible for the tangy, citrus perfume of many Thai soups, salads, stir-fries, and curries. Grated rind goes into curry pastes, larp, and fish cakes. Both are used in some fish and poultry dishes in Indonesia and Malaysia. Always use fresh leaves when available and never use dried in a salad. Whole leaves may be removed from a dish before serving, but if leaves are to be eaten, for example as a garnish for a clear soup, shred them very finely – as fine as a needle – with a small, sharp knife. The leaves keep their flavor well when cooked.

If you buy rind in brine, rinse it well and scrape off the pith before using; shredded, dried rind is best soaked briefly before being added to slow-cooked dishes. The pith makes dried rind bitter, so use sparingly. To give a citrus flavor to a Western dish, use leaves in chicken casseroles, with braised or roasted fish, or in sauces to serve with chicken or fish.

Essential to Thai curry pastes, Indonesian sambals.

Good with fish and seafood, mushrooms, noodles, pork, poultry, rice, green vegetables.

Combines well with Asian basils, chili, cilantro, coconut milk, galangal, ginger, lemon grass, rau ram, sesame, star anise.

Whole fresh fruit
The fruit is pear-shaped, bumpy, and wrinkled, lime green in color, and 2½–3in (7–8cm) long. What little juice it yields is sour and seldom used.

GRATED FRESH RIND
The very thin rind is best removed with a small-holed grater rather than a citrus grater, whose fine perforations will reduce the rind to a mushy mass. Proceed with caution to avoid including the bitter pith.

GALANGAL
Alpinia species

TASTING NOTES

The aroma of greater galangal is mildly gingery and camphorous; the taste has a lemony sourness with a flavor resembling ginger and cardamom mixed. Lesser galangal is more pungent, with a hint of eucalypt; its taste is piquant, suggesting a mix of pepper and ginger.

PARTS USED

Rhizome.

BUYING AND STORING

Fresh greater galangal can be bought from Asian markets, possibly under its local names – it is called kha in Thailand, lengkuas in Malaysia, and laos in Indonesia – or called Laos, Siamese or Thai ginger. It will keep for 2 weeks and can be frozen. Dried slices and powdered galangal (labeled laos) are more widely available. Powdered galangal can be kept for 2 months; slices keep their flavor for at least a year. Galangal in brine can be substituted for fresh; rinse it thoroughly before use. Lesser galangal rhizomes, which are reddish-brown outside and pale red inside, are seldom seen in the US.

HARVESTING

The rhizomes are lifted, cleaned, and processed much like those of turmeric or ginger.

There are two main types of galangal: greater galangal, *A. galanga*, is native to Java; lesser galangal, *A. officinarum*, is native to the coastal regions of southern China. Greater galangal indeed grows taller than lesser and has larger rhizomes. Both are cultivated extensively throughout Southeast Asia, Indonesia, and India. The popularity of lesser galangal has long declined in favor of greater galangal, which continues to be used in the kitchen, principally in Southeast Asia. The English name stems from the Arabic *khalanjan*.

Greater galangal
A. galanga

Whole rhizomes of greater galangal are large and knobby, light orange-brown outside, and marked with darker rings. Young shoots have a pink hue.

SLICED RHIZOME
The flesh is fibrous and buff-colored. Unless very young, the rhizomes are tougher and woodier than those of ginger.

Culinary uses

Throughout Southeast Asia, greater galangal is used fresh in curries and stews, in sambals, satays, soups, and sauces. In Thailand, it is an essential ingredient in some curry powders, as it is in the laksa spices of Malay Nonya cooking. In Thai cooking it is often preferred where other Asian cuisines would use ginger, especially to neutralize the smells of fish and seafood. It is good with chicken and in many hot and sour soups: it provides the key flavoring in tom kha kai, the popular chicken and coconut milk soup.

Like ginger, fresh galangal is easy to peel and grate or chop. It is always preferred to dried, but dried slices can be added to soups and stews; first soak them in hot water for about 30 minutes. They should be taken out before serving because they remain unpleasantly woody to chew. Powdered galangal is used in spice blends throughout the Middle East and across North Africa to Morocco (in ras el hanout). Grated galangal and lime juice are used to make a popular tonic in Southeast Asia. The use of lesser galangal appears to be largely restricted to tonic and healing soups.

Essential to Thai curry pastes.

Good with chicken, fish and seafood.

Combines well with chili, coconut milk, fennel, fish sauces, garlic, ginger, lemon grass, lemon juice, kaffir lime, shallots, tamarind.

SLICED DRIED RHIZOME
Dried slices are satisfactory for flavoring soups and stews and should be soaked in water before use.

GROUND RHIZOME
Tan-colored lesser galangal powder is gingerlike and sharp; greater galangal is sandy-beige, with a sour aroma and a milder ginger flavor.

CITRUS

Citrus species

Citrus fruits are universal providers of tartness in the kitchen. The Japanese use the peel of a small citron, called yuzu; the Chinese favor dried orange or tangerine peel; in the Gulf States and Iran, dried limes are preferred; in Tunisia, bitter orange peel and fruit are used for pickling liquids. In the West, cooks use juice and grated rind for their acidity, and candied peel in desserts and cakes. In the Caribbean islands and Mexico, it would be unthinkable to cook without limes.

Preserved lemons
The chopped peel of salted lemons preserved in their juice is used to flavor Moroccan tagines; it combines particularly well with green olives in a renowned chicken dish. The salty juice is good in salad dressings.

LICORICE

Glycyrrhiza species

Licorice plants are perennial shrubs with blue or lilac, pea-like flowers. The most important species are G. *glabra*, native to southeastern Europe and southwestern Asia; G. *glandulifera*, which grows further east and is known as Russian or Persian licorice; and G. *uralensis*, the main form used in Asia, native to the steppes of northern China. Licorice has been cultivated in Europe for about 1,000 years, in China at least twice as long. It is still used medicinally as a cough-repressant, an expectorant, and a gentle laxative.

PARTS USED

Rhizomes and roots.

BUYING AND STORING

Dried licorice roots can be bought from spice merchants. They keep almost indefinitely if they are quite dry; they can be sliced or ground as needed. Powdered licorice, gray-green and rather strong, needs an airtight container. Sticks and slabs, too, last well if kept dry.

HARVESTING

Licorice plants are easily grown from seed or root cuttings. They need rich, sandy soil and plentiful sun. The roots can be dug up in autumn; drying them takes several months. Roots are usually crushed to a pulp, which manufacturers boil to a thick consistency and reduce further by evaporation. The resulting soluble substance is called extract of licorice. Some manufacturers extract glycyrrhizic acid for use as a flavoring.

Culinary uses

The greatest amount of licorice flavoring is used for tobacco; cough syrups and toothpaste come a distant second. In the form of drinks such as sambuca and pastis the flavor enters a variety of dishes, both sweet and savory. A soft drink is made with it in Islamic countries during Ramadan. In Morocco, the powder flavors snail and octopus dishes and is often an ingredient in ras el hanout. A little licorice improves Chinese five-spice powder; it also flavors Chinese soy sauce.

The Dutch extrude the extract into black, salty licorice, called *drop*, in a bewildering variety of shapes and strengths; the English have multi-colored licorice allsorts and Pontefract cakes – lozenges named after the Yorkshire monastery where they originated in the 16th century. Licorice sticks are popular in Asia for chewing. In Turkey, fresh roots are eaten and powder is used in baking. In the West, licorice is becoming a fashionable flavoring for ice cream.

POWDER
Finely powdered licorice is most readily available from Chinese markets.

SAFFRON
Crocus sativus

TASTING NOTES

The smell of saffron is unmistakable: rich, pungent, musky, floral, honeyed, and tenacious. The taste is delicate yet penetrating, warm, earthy, musky, bitter, and lingering. The aromatic properties vary slightly depending on the saffron's place of origin.

PARTS USED

Stigmas.

BUYING AND STORING

Buy dried stamens (known as filaments or threads); ground saffron is easily adulterated. Threads keep their flavor for 2–3 years if stored in an airtight container in a cool, dark place. Buy saffron only from a reliable source; in tourist markets around the world turmeric, marigold petals, and safflower are passed off as saffron. None has saffron's penetrating aroma, so smell before buying. If you use saffron regularly, buy it in larger quantities from a spice merchant.

HARVESTING

The violet-colored crocus flowers in autumn. The flowers are picked at dawn and the three red stigmas are plucked from each one. Small quantities are toasted on a drum sieve over a low fire. Dried stamens are deep red to orange-red, wiry, and brittle.

Saffron consists of the dried stigmas of the saffron crocus, or roses as they are called. Native to the Mediterranean and western Asia, it was used by the ancient civilizations of the region as a dye and to flavor food and wine. Spain is the main producer; at harvest time on the plain of La Mancha, a heady, sensual aroma explodes around you as the stigmas are toasted. It takes about 80,000 roses to yield 5lb (2.5kg) of stigmas, which produce 1lb (500g) of saffron after toasting. No wonder it is the most expensive spice in the world.

Whole threads

The best-quality saffron is deep red; this is called coupe for Spanish and Kashmiri saffron, sargol for Iranian. A proportion of thicker, yellow threads from the style of the flower is included in the next grade, Mancha if Spanish or Kashmiri, poshal or kayam if Iranian. Good-quality saffron is also produced in Greece and Italy. Lesser grades tend to have a brownish color and stubby, rather untidy threads.

IRANIAN POSHAL
This saffron has deep red, wiry threads with a few yellow styles.

KASHMIRI COUPE
This saffron has a rich, burgundy color. The threads are very long, firm, and smooth.

Culinary uses

Saffron has long been renowned as a dye, whether for the robes of Buddhist monks or for paella and risotto. For most dishes saffron is infused in liquid. If an infusion is added in the early stages of cooking it will impart more color; added at a later stage it contributes more aromatics. Avoid overuse: it can give a bitter, medicinal taste to foods. If a dish does not call for liquid, threads can be ground and stirred in. If they are not quite dry, dry-roast lightly before grinding.

Several cultures flavor specific dishes with saffron, often dishes associated with festivals or celebrations. Saffron provides the characteristic flavor for many Mediterranean fish soups and stews of which Provençal bouillabaisse and Catalan zarzuela are the best known. It adds class to a simple stew of mussels and potatoes or a fish baked in white wine. Saffron rice is excellent whether as a Valencian paella, risotto alla Milanese, an Iranian polo, a Moghul biryani, or a simple vegetable pilaf. In Sweden, saffron buns and cakes are made for the festival of light on December 13, St Lucia's Day. Traditional Cornish saffron cakes and breads have all but disappeared from Britain, but they are not difficult to make and have a fine, rich flavor. Saffron ice cream, whether in the European style, Middle Eastern with mastic, or Indian kulfi, is also worth a try.

Good with asparagus, carrots, chicken, eggs, fish and seafood, leeks, mushrooms, pheasant, rabbit, spinach, winter squashes.

Combines well with anise, cardamom, cinnamon, fennel, ginger, mastic, nutmeg, paprika, pepper, rosebuds, rose water.

SPANISH MANCHA
Spanish Mancha saffron is more orange-red in color with yellow styles.

GROUND THREADS
Ground saffron is easily adulterated with cheaper and inferior spices.

warm and earthy spices

CARDAMOM

Elettaria cardamomum

TASTING NOTES

The aroma of cardamom is strong but mellow, fruity, and penetrating. The taste is lemony and flowery, with a note of camphor or eucalypt due to cineole in the essential oil; it is pungent and smoky, with a warm, bittersweet note, yet is also clean and fresh.

PARTS USED

Dried seeds.

BUYING AND STORING

Pods will keep for a year or more in an airtight jar, but will slowly fade in both color and aroma. Exposed to air, the seeds quickly lose their volatile oils; grinding speeds up the loss. Ground cardamom is easy to adulterate and in any case usually includes the hulls, so it is better to grind your own when needed.

HARVESTING

Fruits ripen from September to December and are harvested at intervals while about three-quarters ripe, otherwise they split open. They are dried in the sun for 3–4 days, or more quickly in drying sheds. Dried pods are hard; the best are green to green-amber. Green pods from Kerala traditionally set the standards of quality and price, but Guatemalan cardamom is nearly as good.

Cardamom is the fruit of a large, perennial bush that grows wild in the rainforests of the Western Ghats (also known as the Cardamon Hills) in southern India; a closely related variety grows in Sri Lanka. Both are now cultivated in their regions of origin and in Tanzania, Vietnam, and Papua New Guinea; Guatemala has become the main exporter. Cardamom has been used in India for some 2,000 years. It reached Europe along the caravan routes, and the Vikings took it from Constantinople to Scandinavia, where it is still very popular.

Whole pods

Cardamom is best bought as whole pods, which should be plump and green. White pods are bleached green ones; less well flavored, their production is declining.

SEEDS

Inside each oval seed pod, triangular in section, are 15–20 tiny, dark brown or black, sticky seeds. Stickiness is the best indication of freshness.

Culinary uses

Cardamom enhances both sweet and savory flavors. In India, it is one of the essential components in many spice mixes. It goes into sweetmeats, pastries, puddings, and ice creams (kulfi), and is used in a digestive and breath-freshening paan with fennel and anise seeds and areca nuts. In India, it is also much used to flavor tea, while in Arab countries coffee is flavored with cardamom, often by pouring it over pods put in the spout of the pot – in Bedouin culture the cardamom used is first displayed to guests, bright green and pristine, as a mark of respect. Cardamom is an essential component of spice mixes in Lebanon, Syria, the Gulf States (baharat), and Ethiopia (berbere). Scandinavia is still the biggest importer in Europe; there and in Germany and Russia, cardamom is widely used for spiced cakes, pastries, and breads, and occasionally also in hamburgers and meat loaf.

Whole pods, lightly crushed, can be used to flavor rice, poached and braised dishes, and casseroles. They are an important ingredient in many Indian slow-braised meat dishes (kormas), which use a thick marinating liquid to develop a creamy sauce. Hulled seeds can be either lightly bruised and fried, or toasted and ground, before being added to a dish. Cardamom is good in baked apples, poached pears, and fruit salads. It combines well with orange and coffee in desserts, but is equally at home with roast duck or poached chicken, in marinades or spiced wine. It is useful in pickles.

Essential to berbere, curry powders, dals, masalas, pilafs, Indian rice pudding (kheer), zhug.

Good with apples, oranges, pears; legumes, sweet potatoes, and other root vegetables.

Combines well with caraway, chili, cinnamon, cloves, coffee, coriander, cumin, ginger, paprika, pepper, saffron, yogurt.

Spices for pilafs

Indian pilafs are flavored with whole spices, including green cardamom pods, pieces of cinnamon, cloves, cumin seed, and black peppercorns, which are simply added to the rice before it is cooked.

BLACK CARDAMOM
Amomum and Aframomum species

The seeds of several species of *Amomum* and *Aframomum* are widely used in the regions where they are grown, and sometimes they are sold, ground, as cheap substitutes for green cardamom. In color they are various shades of brown and their taste is usually more camphorous than that of green cardamom. The most important is Greater Indian or Nepal cardamom, *Amomum subulatum*, native to the eastern Himalayas. This particular variety, usually referred to as black cardamom, is never used as a substitute for green cardamom and has a distinct and separate role in Indian cooking.

PARTS USED

Dried seeds.

BUYING AND STORING

Buy pods that are whole, not broken, and store in an airtight container.

HARVESTING

Harvesting takes place from August to November, somewhat earlier than that of green cardamom (*p.128*), and drying is always done in sheds. The resulting color is a very dark brown.

Culinary uses

In contrast to green cardamom, which is considered a "cooling" spice, black cardamom is a "heating" spice. It is therefore an important ingredient in combination with cloves, cinnamon, and black pepper in any garam masala, the hot spice mixture that can be used either at the start of cooking or sprinkled over for a stronger effect toward the end. Black cardamom also occasionally finds its way into confectionery and pickles. When pods are used whole in vegetable or meat stews they should be removed before serving.

Essential to garam masala.
Good with pilafs and other rice dishes, meat and vegetable curries.
Combines well with ajowan, green cardamom, cassia leaves, chili, cinnamon, cloves, coriander, cumin, nutmeg, pepper, yogurt.

ZEDOARY

Curcuma species

Native to subtropical wet forest zones of Southeast Asia and Indonesia, zedoary was brought to Europe in the 6th century, and used in medicines and perfume. During the Middle Ages it became popular in the kitchen alongside galangal; its culinary use is now largely restricted to Southeast Asia. Increased European interest in the food of that region has led to the availability of fresh zedoary, but the dried spice remains almost unknown.

TASTING NOTES

Fresh zedoary has a pleasant, musky taste somewhat similar to young ginger, clean and crisp with a hint of bitterness. *C. zerumbet* is increasingly available in fresh form. Combine with other fresh spices or use as a crisp garnish. The brown skin is removed before use.

PARTS USED

Fresh or dried rhizome; young shoots, flowerbuds, and leaves.

BUYING AND STORING

Fresh zedoary is available from Asian markets, often as "white turmeric." It has a thin, brown skin and lemon-colored, crisp flesh. It keeps in the refrigerator for 2 weeks. Dried zedoary slices can also be bought in Asian markets. The spice is often available ground; the powder is usually colored reddish-brown artificially.

HARVESTING

The fleshy, yellow rhizomes take 2 years to reach full development. Then they are lifted and sold fresh, or boiled or steamed, cut into slices, and dried. Dried slices are grayish-brown, hard, and have a rough, somewhat hairy texture.

Culinary uses

In Indonesia, young zedoary shoots are eaten and the flowerbuds are used in salads; the long, aromatic leaves wrap and flavor fish. In Thailand, peeled and shredded or finely sliced fresh zedoary is added to salads or raw vegetables to serve with nam prik. In Mumbai, a fresh zedoary and vegetable soup is popular. Chopped fresh zedoary mixed with shallots, fresh lemon grass, and cilantro makes a good spice paste for cooking vegetables in coconut milk. In Southeast Asia, dried zedoary is used in the preparation of curries and condiments, and in dishes for which dried turmeric or dried ginger might be used. It goes well with chicken and lamb in southern Indian and Indonesian dishes.

Good with chickpeas, curries and stews, fish, lentils, poultry, Asian soups, green vegetables.

Combines well with chili, cilantro, coconut milk, garlic, ginger, kaffir lime leaves, lemon grass, turmeric.

TURMERIC

Curcuma longa

A member of the ginger family, turmeric is a robust perennial, native to southern Asia and appreciated there since antiquity as a flavoring, a dye, and a medicine. It is one of the cheapest spices, yet throughout the region it is valued on ritual and ceremonial occasions, whether to color rice for an Indonesian wedding or to dye the skin of cows (as I once saw during the Sankali festival in Mysore). India is the main producer of turmeric and more than 90 percent of the crop is used domestically. Other producers include China, Haiti, Indonesia, Jamaica, Malaysia, Pakistan, Peru, Sri Lanka, and Vietnam.

Whole fresh rhizome
Fresh turmeric should be firm and plump. The rhizomes are used sliced, chopped, or grated.

SLICED FRESH RHIZOME
Add pared, sliced turmeric to pickles and relishes; it has a wonderful color and taste, and is also a preservative.

Culinary uses

Turmeric binds and harmonizes the other spices with which it appears in many combinations. Use it sparingly. Fresh turmeric is used throughout Southeast Asia in spice pastes made with lemon grass, galangal, garlic, shallots, tamarind, chili peppers, and sometimes dried shrimp paste and candlenuts. Chopped or grated, it goes into laksas, stews, and vegetable dishes. Juice extracted from crushed turmeric flavors and colors rice dishes for festive meals in Indonesia and Malaysia. The fragrant leaves are used to wrap foods in Malaysia, and the shoots are eaten as a vegetable in Thailand.

In India and the West Indies, dried, ground turmeric combined with other spices is the basis of masalas, curry powders, and pastes. It imparts a warm flavor and yellow-orange color to many regional vegetable, bean, and lentil dishes. It occurs in North African tagines and stews, most notably in the Moroccan spice blend ras el hanout, and in harira, the national soup. In Iran, turmeric and dried limes flavor gheimeh, a rich stew-sauce that is spooned over rice.

In the West, turmeric is used as a colorant for cheese, margarine, and some mustards. It is widely used in pickles and relishes of both eastern and western manufacture.

Essential to masalas, curry powders and pastes, ras el hanout.

Good with beans, eggplant, eggs, fish, lentils, meat, poultry, rice, root vegetables, spinach.

Combines well with chili, cilantro, cloves, coconut milk, coriander, cumin, curry leaf, fennel, galangal, garlic, ginger, kaffir lime leaves, lemon grass, mustard seeds, paprika, pepper, rau ram.

GRATED DRIED RHIZOME
Turmeric stains fingers, utensils, and clothes, so be careful when using it.

WHOLE DRIED RHIZOME
Dried rhizomes look like tough, yellow wood; they are almost impossible to grind at home, but can be grated.

CUMIN

Cuminum cyminum

TASTING NOTES

The smell of cumin is strong and heavy, spicy-sweet, with acrid but warm depth. The flavor is rich, slightly bitter, sharp, earthy, and warm, with a persistent pungency. Use sparingly.

PARTS USED

Dried seeds (fruits).

BUYING AND STORING

Cumin seeds are widely available, either whole or ground. Black cumin can be bought from Asian markets, as can dhana-jeera, a blend of cumin and coriander seeds. Seeds will keep their pungency in an airtight jar for several months, but ground cumin has a very short shelf life.

HARVESTING

Cumin stems are cut when the plants begin to wither and the seeds turn brown; they are threshed and the seeds dried in the sun. In many countries the harvest is still done manually.

Cumin is the seed of a small, herbaceous umbellifer, native to just one locality, the Nile valley of Egypt, but long cultivated in most hot regions – the eastern Mediterranean, North Africa, India, China, and the Americas. It was used in medicines in Egypt and Minoan Crete at least 4,000 years ago. The Romans used it the way we use pepper. During the Middle Ages cumin was popular in Europe, but gradually caraway took its place. Spanish explorers took it to Latin America, where it is has become a very popular spice.

Whole seeds

Cumin seeds are oval, brownish-green in color, about ¼in (5mm) long. They look like caraway but are straighter and show a characteristic pattern of longitudinal ridges.

GROUND SEEDS
For the best flavor, only grind seed as needed.

Culinary uses

The aroma of cumin is enhanced if the seeds are dry-roasted before they are ground, or fried in oil if they are used whole. Early Spanish dishes combined cumin, saffron, and anise seed or cinnamon. Now cumin is found in Moroccan couscous, in the merguez sausages of North Africa, in Tex-Mex chile con carne, and more sparingly in the spice mixes of Mexico itself. It is added to pretzels in Alsace, pork sausages in Portugal, cheese in Holland, pickled cabbage in Germany, the tapas known as Moorish kebabs (pinchitos morunos) in Spain, fish dishes in Lebanon, köfte in Turkey, and a pomegranate and walnut sauce in Syria. In all countries that like spicy food it is used in breads, chutneys, relishes, savory spice mixes, and meat or vegetable stews. It is present in curry powders and masalas, and in commercial chili powders. The combination of ground cumin and coriander gives much Indian food its characteristic pungent smell – although authentic Indian recipes can confuse the user because the word for cumin, *jeera*, is sometimes wrongly translated as caraway.

Essential to Iranian advieh, baharat, berbere, Cajun spice blend, curry powders, dukka, masalas, panch phoron, sambhar powder, zhug.

Good with beans, bread, cabbage, hard or pungent cheeses, chicken, eggplant, lamb, lentils, onions, potatoes, rice, sauerkraut, squash.

Combines well with ajowan, allspice, anise seed, bay, cardamom, chili, cinnamon, cloves, coriander, curry leaves, fennel seed, fenugreek seed, garlic, ginger, mace and nutmeg, mustard seed, oregano, paprika, pepper, thyme, turmeric.

Other cumins

True black cumin (*kala jeera*) is an expensive variety grown in Kashmir, northern Pakistan, and Iran. It is used there and in the Gulf States in the same way as ordinary cumin is used elsewhere. Black cumin should not be confused with two other spices sometimes given that name, *Nigella sativa* and *Bunium persicum*; the latter grows wild in the Middle East and is used locally.

Whole black seeds

Darker than ordinary cumin seeds, black cumin seeds are also smaller. They have a sweeter smell and a complex, mellow flavor that is somewhere between cumin and caraway. Dry-roasted seeds go into pilafs and breads.

CARAWAY

Carum carvi

Caraway has a pungent aroma that, like the flavor, is warm and bittersweet, sharply spicy, with a note of dried orange peel and a slight but lingering hint of anise.

PARTS USED

Dried seeds (fruits).

BUYING AND STORING

Caraway seed can be bought ground, but is often used whole and is best bought that way: the seed will keep for at least 6 months in an airtight jar. The seed is easy to grind or pound when needed, but once ground it will lose strength quite quickly.

HARVESTING

Stems are cut when the fruit is ripening, dried for 7–10 days to complete the ripening, then threshed. In the home garden, caraway plants can be grown from seed in well-drained soil in full sun. Their own seeds will not ripen until the second year. Cut ripe seed clusters early in the morning when dew is on them, or the seeds may scatter too freely and the plant will self-seed. To dry, hang up the stems with a paper bag tied around the seedheads.

Caraway is a hardy umbellifer native to Asia and northern and central Europe. It is cultivated as a biennial, not only in its regions of origin but also in Morocco, the US, and Canada. The Romans used it with vegetables and fish, medieval cooks as a flavoring for soups and bean or cabbage dishes. In 17th-century England, it was popular in bread, cakes, and baked fruit; coated with sugar the seeds made comfits. Nowadays Holland and Germany are the major producers. The essential oil flavors spirits such as aquavit and Kümmel.

Whole seeds
The fruit splits into two curved seeds with tapered ends; the hard, brown shell has five lighter-colored ridges.

Culinary uses

In central Europe, and especially in the Jewish cooking originating there, caraway is used to flavor brown or rye breads, crackers, seedcakes, sausages, cabbage, soups, and stews. It gives many south German and Austrian dishes their characteristic flavor, be it pumpernickel bread or roast pork; it is used in coleslaw and in combination with juniper for sauerkraut. It accompanies Munster cheese in Alsace; the seeds are also used in Geromé, another local cheese, and in pain d'épices.

Caraway is used in the cooking of North Africa, mostly in vegetable dishes and in spice blends, such as Tunisian tabil and harissa. Morocco has a traditional caraway soup – as does Hungary, where caraway also figures prominently in goulash. Mention of caraway in Indian recipes usually stems from a mistranslation of the word for cumin; caraway itself is used only in northern India – it grows wild in the Himalayas. Turkish recipes may cite "black caraway," which is not true caraway but nigella (*p.89*).

Young leaves, less pungent than the seeds and resembling dill in taste and appearance, are an interesting addition to salads, soups, or fresh white cheese. They make a good garnish for lightly cooked young vegetables and most other dishes for which parsley could be used.

Essential to tabil, harissa.

Good with apples, breads, cabbage, duck, goose, noodles, onions, pork, potatoes and other root vegetables, sauerkraut, tomatoes.

Combines well with coriander, garlic, juniper, parsley, thyme.

Tunisian tabil spices

Used for stews and vegetable and beef dishes, tabil is a blend of caraway seeds, coriander seeds, garlic, and chili.

NUTMEG

Myristica fragrans

TASTING NOTES

Nutmeg and mace have a similar rich, fresh, and warm aroma. Nutmeg smells sweet but is more camphorous and pine-like than mace. The taste of both is warm and highly aromatic, but nutmeg has hints of clove and a deeper, bittersweet, woody flavor.

This spreading, evergreen tree, native to the Banda islands of Indonesia, often called the Spice Islands, produces fruit that yields two distinct spices, nutmeg and mace (*p.140*). In the 6th century both spices formed part of the caravan trade to Alexandria; they were probably taken to Europe by the crusaders. Their early use, in China, India, Arabia, and Europe alike, was medicinal. When the Portuguese started trading direct from the islands, nutmeg gained importance as a spice, and by the 18th century a real craze for it developed in England.

PARTS USED

Kernel of the seed.

BUYING AND STORING

Nutmeg is best bought whole. In airtight containers it keeps almost indefinitely and is easily ground or grated as required. Once ground, nutmeg loses its flavor rather quickly. Banda and Penang nutmeg and mace are considered to be superior to the West Indian ones.

HARVESTING

The yellowish, apricot-like fruits are gathered when ripe and the outer skin, white flesh, and mace are stripped off. The seeds, covered by a hard brown-black shell, are dried on trays for 6–8 weeks, until the kernel – the nutmeg – rattles in its shell. The shells are then cracked open and the smooth, brown nutmegs are removed and graded by size. The yield of nutmeg is about ten times that of mace, which makes the latter comparatively costly.

Whole seeds
Nutmeg seeds can be bought intact, with the kernel still inside its hard shell, and the lacy aril still clinging to the shell.

NUTMEG
The hard, outer shells are stripped from the kernels and discarded.

Culinary uses

In India, nutmeg is used more than mace because of the latter's high cost; both are used sparingly, mainly in Moghul dishes. The Arabs have long used both spices in delicately flavored mutton and lamb dishes. In North Africa, they are found in such spice mixtures as Tunisian qâlat daqqa and Moroccan ras el hanout. The Europeans have used nutmeg and mace most extensively, in both sweet and savory dishes.

Nutmeg is widely used in honey cakes, rich fruit cakes, fruit desserts, and fruit punch. It goes well in stews and in most egg and cheese dishes, as does mace. The Dutch add nutmeg lavishly to white cabbage, cauliflower, vegetable purées, meat stews, and fruit puddings; the Italians add rather more subtle quantities to mixed vegetable dishes, spinach, veal, and fillings or sauces for pasta. In France, it is used with pepper and cloves in slow-cooked stews and ragoûts. Half-ripe nutmeg, pricked all over (as is done with unripe walnuts) and soaked before being boiled twice in syrup, was once a popular sweetmeat from Malaysia.

In very large quantities nutmeg's hallucinogenic properties become toxic; drinking alcohol greatly increases the harmful effect.

Essential to baking or dessert spices, quatre épices, ras el hanout, Tunisian five spices.

Good with cabbage, carrots, cheese and cheese dishes, chicken, eggs, fish and seafood chowders, lamb, milk dishes, onion, potato, pumpkin pie, spinach, sweet potato, veal.

Combines well with cardamom, cinnamon, cloves, coriander, cumin, rose geranium, ginger, mace, pepper, rosebuds, thyme.

GRATED NUTMEG
Nutmeg kernels are best kept whole and only grated when needed. Some graters (*below*) have a lidded compartment in which the kernels can be stored.

MACE

Myristica fragrans

Inside the apricot-like fruit of *Myristica fragrans* lies a hard seed, the kernel of which is the spice nutmeg (*p.138*). Around this seed is a lacy covering or aril; this is the second spice, mace. Both nutmeg and mace became important commodities in a trade started by the Portuguese in the 16th century, developed by the Dutch, and taken over by the English when they captured the Spice Islands in 1796. Planting began in Penang, Sri Lanka, Sumatra, and the West Indies, where Grenada now produces almost a third of the world's crop.

TASTING NOTES

Mace has nutmeg's rich, fresh, and warm aroma, but the smell is stronger and shows a lively, floral character with notes of pepper and clove. The taste of mace is warm, aromatic, delicate, and subtle with some lemony sweetness, yet it finishes with a potent bitterness.

PARTS USED

Aril surrounding the seed.

BUYING AND STORING

Ground mace is more commonly available than whole pieces (the pieces are called blades), but the latter are worth seeking out. They keep almost indefinitely in an airtight container and can be ground in a spice mill.

HARVESTING

The ripe fruit of nutmeg trees is collected and the outer skin and white flesh removed to reveal the seed. The thin, leathery, lacy, bright scarlet aril, the mace, that covers the seed is removed, pressed flat, and dried for a few hours only. Mace from Grenada is then stored in the dark for about 4 months, during which time it turns a deep orange-yellow; Indonesian mace remains orange-red.

Mace and nutmeg
Produced by the same tree, these spices are similar in taste. Mace is preferred when the dish requires a lighter flavoring.

BLADES
Mace blades are brittle, yet they exude oil when pressed with the fingernails.

GROUND BLADES
Ground mace keeps its flavor reasonably well, longer than some other ground spices.

Culinary uses

In Southeast Asia and China, mace and nutmeg are used more for their medical than for culinary properties. Elsewhere mace and nutmeg tend to be used interchangeably by cooks, although nutmeg is more widely used because it is cheaper.

Mace gives a lift to béchamel and onion sauces, clear soups, shellfish stock, potted meat, cheese soufflés, chocolate drinks, and cream cheese desserts. Mace should be used in preference to nutmeg to preserve the delicate color of a dish. Whole blades of mace can be used to flavor soups and stews, but should be removed before serving.

In Indonesia, after the mace and kernel have been removed from the nutmeg fruit, the outer flesh is candied. In Sulawesi, in particular, it is cured in the sun and sprinkled with palm sugar, whereupon it becomes almost translucent.

Essential to pickling spices.

Good with cabbage, carrots, cheese and cheese dishes, chicken, egg dishes, fish and seafood chowders, lamb, milk dishes, onion, pâtés and terrines, potato, pumpkin pie, spinach, sweet potato, veal.

Combines well with cardamom, cinnamon, cloves, coriander, cumin, rose geranium, ginger, nutmeg, paprika, pepper, rosebuds, thyme.

Aromatic garam masala

Cardamom subtly dominates the flavor of this mild masala blend, made from green or black cardamom, cinnamon, mace, black peppercorns, and cloves.

ACHIOTE

Bixa orellana

Achiote is the orange-red seed of the small evergreen annatto tree, native to tropical South America. In pre-Columbian times the seeds were already widely used as a colorant for food, fabrics, and body paint; in the Western world they are still used as such in butter, cheese, smoked fish, and in cosmetics. Brazil and the Philippines are the main producers, but the tree grows throughout Central America, the Caribbean, and in parts of Asia. Also sometimes called annatto seed, achiote is its name in the Nahuatl language of Mexico.

TASTING NOTES

The seeds have a faint flowery or peppermint scent, and a delicate, earthy, slightly peppery taste with a hint of bitterness. They impart an agreeably earthy taste to food if used in quantities much larger than those required for coloring only.

PARTS USED

Dried seeds.

BUYING AND STORING

Achiote seeds are available, whole or ground, from Latin American, Spanish and East Indian markets. Seeds should be a healthy rust-red; avoid any that are dull and brownish. Powdered achiote is often mixed with cornstarch, sometimes with other spices such as cumin. Seeds and powder should be kept in an airtight jar out of the light. Seeds will keep for at least 3 years.

HARVESTING

The large, rose-like flowers develop into prickly, orange-red pods at the end of the branches; each contains about 50 brick-red, angular seeds. When ripe the pods are harvested, split open, and macerated in water. The pulp embedding the seeds is pressed into cakes for processing into dyes; the seeds are dried as a spice.

GROUND SEEDS
Dried achiote seeds are very hard and are most easily ground in an electric spice mill.

Whole dried seeds

Whole seeds are mostly used as a colorant. Soak ½ tsp in 1 tbsp boiling water for 1 hour, or until the water is a deep orange color.

Culinary uses

Achiote seeds can be soaked in hot water to obtain a colored liquid for stocks and stews, or to color rice. In the Caribbean, the seeds are fried in fat, over low heat, then discarded before the now deep-golden or orange fat is used for cooking. The fat, or oil treated the same way, can be stored in a sealed glass jar in the refrigerator for several months.

In Jamaica, achiote may be used with onion and chili peppers in the sauce for saltfish and ackee, often called the national dish. In the Philippines, achiote is ground and added to soups and stews, mostly for color effect; it is an essential ingredient in the famous pork-and-chicken dish, pipián. In Peru, it is used in marinades, especially for pork. In Venezuela, it is combined with garlic, paprika, and herbs to make a popular condiment called aliño criollo. In Mexico, it goes into achiote paste – the Yucatán recado rojo – basis of the region's best-known dish, pollo pibil (marinated chicken wrapped in banana leaves and cooked in a pit oven); the paste is equally good spread on fish or pork before grilling. In Mexico, achiote is also sometimes added to the dough for tamales, the stuffed cornmeal-paste rolls steamed in a corn-husk wrapping. In Vietnam, cooks use oil dyed with achiote as the base of braised dishes to give them color.

Essential to pipián, recado rojo.
Good with beef, egg dishes, fish (especially salt cod), legumes, okra, onions, pork, poultry, rice, squash, sweet peppers, sweet potatoes, tomatoes, most vegetables.
Combines well with allspice, chili, citrus juice, cloves, cumin, epazote, garlic, oregano, paprika, peanuts.

Recado rojo

Red achiote paste is indispensable to the cooking of Mexico's Yucatán peninsula. Achiote seeds are combined with black peppercorns, cloves, cumin and coriander seeds, dried oregano, garlic, and bitter orange juice or wine vinegar. Small hot red chili peppers may be added.

CURRY LEAVES

Murraya koenigii

Curry leaves come from a small, deciduous tree that grows wild in the foothills of the Himalayas, in many parts of India, northern Thailand, and Sri Lanka. The tree has been cultivated in southern India for centuries; plantations have also been established in northern Australia.

Culinary uses

Curry leaves are stripped from the stems just before they are added to the dish. They are used extensively in the cooking of south India, much as cilantro is used in the north. They are used in Gujarati vegetable dishes, meat stews and the fish curries of Kerala and Chennai (Madras) where they are often used in spice mixes.

Sri Lankan curry mixtures also routinely include curry leaves. These mixtures are darker in appearance and taste than the Indian ones: the ingredients are more highly toasted. Indian emigrants took curry leaves to Fiji, while others made them an important ingredient in South African Tamil cooking.

Leaves impart a delicate, spicy flavour to curries without the heat often associated with those dishes.

Fresh leaves

The slender stalks may have as many as 20 small, bright green leaves.

CAPERS

Capparis species

The caper bush is a small shrub that grows wild all around the Mediterranean, as far south as the Sahara and as far east as northern Iran, although it may have originated in dry regions of western and central Asia.

Culinary uses

Capers are an important ingredient in many sauces, such as ravigote, remoulade, tartar, and salsa alla puttanesca. English caper sauce, once traditional with mutton, is equally good with firm fish. Salt cod with capers and green olives, is a standard combination for fish dishes in Sicily; in Spain, with fried fish, capers are combined with almonds, garlic, and parsley. Black olives and capers are the basis of tapenade. In Hungary and Austria, they flavor Liptauer cheese. Both capers and caper berries can be eaten on their own, like olives, or used as a relish with cold meats, smoked fish, and cheese. Used with discretion they can liven up a salad.

Pickled or salted capers should be rinsed before use. When capers are used in cooked dishes they should be added toward the end as lengthy cooking tends to bring out an undesirable, bitter flavor.

Essential to tapenade, various sauces.

Good with artichokes, eggplant, fish, green beans, gherkins, lamb, olives, potatoes, poultry, seafood.

Combines well with anchovies, arugula, basil, celery, garlic, lemon, mustard, olives, oregano, parsley, tarragon.

TASTING NOTES

The taste of pickled capers (once the vinegar or salt is rinsed off) is piquant, fresh, salty, and somewhat lemony. The pungency in its flavor derives mainly from a mustard oil, glycoside, not unlike those found in horseradish and wasabi.

PARTS USED

Unopened flowerbuds; unripe fruits.

BUYING AND STORING

Capers from southern France are graded from nonpareilles to capottes, according to size – the smaller ones being the best. Other important producers are Cyprus, Malta, Italy, Spain, and California. Pickled capers keep for a long time provided they are kept covered by the pickling liquid, which should not be renewed or added to, least of all with vinegar.

HARVESTING

Caper buds are picked by hand when they are the right size, wilted for a day or two, graded to size, then put in vinegar or dry-salted. The intensely flavored, large, Sicilian capers are always dry-salted, as are top-quality small ones. Salting preserves taste and texture better than pickling does.

Capers
Capers are pickled in vinegar or dry-salted. Quality depends on place of origin, preserving method, and their size.

bitter or astringent spices

FENUGREEK

Trigonella foenum-graecum

Native to western Asia and southeastern Europe, fenugreek has a long
history of use as a flavoring and medicine. The Latin name *Trigonella*
refers to the triangular shape of the seeds, and *foenum-graecum* means
Greek hay, a reference to its use as a fodder crop in classical times, a
use for which it is still better known in Europe today.

Culinary uses

A good source of protein, minerals, and
vitamins, fenugreek is widely used by
vegetarians in India. They make extensive
use of fresh fenugreek (methi) leaves as a
vegetable, cooked with potatoes, spinach,
or rice. The leaves are also chopped and
added to the dough for naans and
chapattis. Dried leaves are used to flavor
sauces and gravies. Fresh or dried leaves
are essential to the classic Iranian herb
and lamb stew, ghormeh sabzi.

Seeds are used in Indian pickles and
chutney, in the southern spice blend
sambhar powder, and in panch phoron
from Bengal. They are much used in dals
and fish curries in the south, and ground

with flour to make the local dosai breads.
In Egypt and Ethiopia, fenugreek also
flavors breads, and it is a constituent
of Ethiopian berbere spice mixture. In
Turkey and Armenia, ground fenugreek
is combined with chili and garlic and
rubbed onto pastirma, the excellent dried
beef of the region.

Essential to sambhar powder, panch
phoron, berbere.

Good with fish curries, green and root
vegetables, lamb, legumes, potatoes,
rice, tomatoes.

Combines well with cardamom,
cinnamon, cloves, coriander, cumin,
fennel seed, garlic, dried limes, nigella,
pepper, turmeric.

WHOLE SEEDS

Brief dry-roasting or frying mellows the flavor
of the seeds and gives them a nutty, burnt-
sugar or maple-syrup taste, but do not heat
for too long or the bitterness is intensified.

AJOWAN
Trachyspermum ammi

TASTING NOTES

When crushed, ajowan seeds have a strong, rather crude smell of thyme. The taste, largely determined by thymol in the essential oil, is hot and bitter. If chewed on their own, ajowan seeds numb the tongue.

PARTS USED

Dried seeds.

BUYING AND STORING

Ajowan can be bought from Indian markets, where it may also be called ajwain or carom. The seeds will keep indefinitely in an airtight jar. Bruise them before use to release their flavor; they are easily ground in a mortar.

HARVESTING

Ajowan stems are cut in May or June, when the seeds are ripe; they are dried, then threshed.

Ajowan, native to southern India, is a small, annual umbellifer closely related to caraway and cumin. The seeds are a popular spice throughout India, and the plant is also grown and used in Pakistan, Afghanistan, Iran, and Egypt.

Culinary uses

Ajowan should be used judiciously: too much will make a dish taste bitter. Cooking mellows the flavor to resemble that of thyme or oregano, but stronger and with a peppery note.

Ajowan has a natural affinity with starchy foods, and in southwestern Asia is used in breads (paratha) and fried snacks (especially those made with chickpea flour). Cooked with dried beans it helps relieve flatulence. It is also used to flavour pickles and root vegetables and in some curry mixes. It is very popular in the vegetarian cuisine of Gujarat, where it is used in batters for bhajias and pakoras, and with chili peppers and cilantro to flavor the crêpes called pudlas. In northern India, ajowan is fried in ghee with other spices before being added to a dish. Probably its best-known use in the West is in the flavoring of a crunchy snack called Bombay mix.

Essential to berbere, chat masala.
Good with fish, green beans, legumes, root vegetables.
Combines well with cardamom, cinnamon, cloves, cumin, fennel seed, garlic, ginger, pepper, turmeric.

Whole seeds
The seeds are small, ridged ovals, grayish-green to reddish-brown, and resemble celery seeds.

MASTIC

Prunus mahaleb

Mastic is a resin produced by cutting the bark of one variety of lentisk tree native to the Greek island of Chios. The tree has many veins, rich in mastic, just beneath the bark of the trunk. The pieces of resin, some oval, some oblong, are called tears. They are semi-transparent, with a light, golden color. Mastic has a brittle texture, but when chewed it takes on the consistency of chewing gum.

PARTS USED

Tears of dried resin. Mastic is powdered before use so that it blends evenly into a dish.

BUYING AND STORING

Mastic is expensive and is sold in small quantities, but you need only a small amount at a time. It is available from Greek and Middle Eastern markets and from spice merchants. Store in a cool place.

HARVESTING

The slow-growing evergreen trees start to produce mastic when 5–6 years old, and continue producing for another 50–60 years. Mastic is harvested from July to October. The gnarled trunks are cut diagonally and the sticky resin oozes out; some collects on the trunk, some falls to the ground. In contact with the air the resin hardens into "tears," which are collected, washed, then cleaned by hand and laid out to dry.

Culinary uses

Mastic's main use is in baking, desserts, and sweetmeats. Greeks use mastic to flavor festive breads, especially the Easter bread tsoureki, and Cypriots in their Easter cheese pastries, flaounes. Most of the crop is exported to Turkey and the Arab states. With sugar and rose or orange-flower water, mastic is used to flavor milk puddings, dried fruit and nut fillings for pastries, Turkish delight, and preserves.

It gives a pleasant, chewy texture to ice creams. Mastic soup, mastic stew, and a mastic sweetmeat are made in Izmir, the Turkish port city in sight of Chios. **Good with** almonds, apricots, fresh cheese, dates, milk desserts, pistachio nuts, rose water and orange-flower water, walnuts. **Combines well with** allspice, cardamom, cinnamon, cloves, mahlab, nigella, poppy seed, sesame.

Mastic tears
Used as a breath-freshener and digestive aid, mastic was the original chewing gum.

PEPPER

Piper nigrum

The history of the spice trade is essentially about the quest for pepper. Peppercorns and long pepper from India's Malabar coast reached Europe at least 3,000 years ago; trade routes were fiercely protected, empires were built and destroyed because of it. In 408AD the Goths demanded pepper as part of their tribute when they laid siege to Rome; later, pepper was traded ounce for ounce for gold, and used as currency to pay rents, dowries, and taxes. In volume and value pepper remains the most important spice. India, Indonesia, Brazil, Malaysia, and Vietnam are the main producers.

TASTING NOTES

Black pepper has a fine, fruity, pungent fragrance with warm, woody, and lemony notes. The taste is hot and biting with a clean, penetrating aftertaste. White pepper is less aromatic, and can smell musty, but it has a sharp pungency with a sweetish afternote.

PARTS USED

Immature and ripe fruits.

BUYING AND STORING

Sun-drying is preferable for peppercorns: if dried at high temperatures in artificial heat some of the volatile oils are lost. Black and white pepper rapidly lose their aroma and flavor when ground, so it is best to buy whole berries and grind in a pepper mill or crush in a mortar, as needed. In airtight containers peppercorns will keep for a year.

HARVESTING

To produce black pepper, immature green berries are picked, briefly fermented, and then dried. During drying the pepper shrivels, becomes wrinkled, and turns black or dark brown. For white peppercorns, berries are picked when yellowish-red and almost ripe, then soaked to soften and loosen the outer skin. Once this is removed they are rinsed and sun-dried.

Whole peppercorns
Large, uniform, dark brown to black peppercorns command the highest price. Aroma and flavor are more important than pungency. The best white pepper is considered to be Muntok from Indonesia.

CRUSHED PEPPER
Crushed peppercorns can be pressed into steaks to be grilled, and release their flavors in marinades.

GROUND PEPPER
Ground white pepper is more attractive in creamy sauces than black.

Pepper has different characteristics in different places of origin and is therefore classified according to where it is grown. Broadly speaking, the flavor of pepper is determined by its essential oil content, while its content of the alkaloid piperine accounts for its bite. Black pepper has both aroma and pungency. White pepper contains less essential oil than black because the oil is present in the hull and is removed in cleaning; that also explains why white pepper, although pungent, has little aroma. Over time the strength of the flavor compounds in the essential oil diminishes. The essential oil and piperine content varies according to the origins of the pepper. Pepper of the best quality is Indian Malabar; it has a fruity aroma and a clean bite. Tellicherry is the grade with the largest berries. Indonesian lampong pepper has more piperine and less essential oil, so it is more pungent than aromatic; the berries are smaller and gray-black in color. Sarawak pepper from Malaysia has a milder aroma than Indonesian berries, but is hot and biting. Brazilian pepper has a low piperine content and is rather bland. Vietnamese is light in color and mild.

RED PEPPERCORNS
Red or pink peppercorns are fully ripe fruits, usually available preserved in brine or vinegar. They have a soft outer shell with a delicate, almost sweet, fruity taste. The inner core provides a moderate, lingering heat.

GREEN PEPPERCORNS
Green pepper has a light aroma, and an agreeable, fresh pungency; it is not overpoweringly hot. Green peppercorns are preserved by freeze-drying or dehydration, or packed in brine or vinegar. Keep fresh green and red pepper berries in the refrigerator.

Culinary uses

Pepper is neither sweet nor savory, merely pungent. Although mostly used in savory foods, it can be used with fruits and in some sweet breads and cakes. It brings out the flavor of other spices and retains its own flavor well during cooking.

The aroma of black pepper can be detected in foods all round the world. Even the chili lovers of Latin America and southern Asia reach for the peppercorns to flavor cooking liquids, stocks, salad dressings, and sauces, or crush them to add to spice mixtures and marinades. Ground pepper is rubbed on fish and meat

to be grilled or baked; it flavors rich stews and curries; and it is used to season simple buttered vegetables and smoked fish.

White pepper is used in pale sauces and cream soups to preserve their attractive appearance. Use it judiciously because the bite is sharp.

In France, mignonette pepper, a mixture consisting of black and white peppercorns, black for aroma and white for strength, is often used.

Rinse brined peppercorns before using. Green pepper combines beautifully with sweeter spices, such as cinnamon, ginger, bay, fennel seed, and lemon grass, to

flavor pork, chicken (rub butter mixed with crushed peppercorns and ginger under the skin before roasting), lobster, crab, and fish, especially salmon. It also makes an excellent steak au poivre and combines well with Dijon mustard. Red peppercorns can be used in similar ways.

Essential to baharat, berbere, garam masala, ras el hanout, quatre épices.
Good with most foods.
Combines well with basil, cardamom, cinnamon, cloves, coconut milk, coriander, cumin, garlic, ginger, lemon, lime, nutmeg, parsley, rosemary, thyme, turmeric.

Mignonette pepper

Black and white *P. nigrum* peppercorns are combined in this French seasoning.

Long pepper *P. longum* and *P. retrofactum*

The long pepper species *P. longum* and *P. retrofactum* originated in India and Indonesia respectively. Long pepper is mostly used in Asia, East Africa, and North Africa in slow-cooked dishes and pickles. The spikes of minute fruits are

harvested green and sun-dried, when they resemble gray-black catkins. Long pepper is usually used whole. It smells sweetly fragrant, and initially resembles black pepper in taste, but it has a biting, numbing aftertaste. Indonesian long pepper is slightly longer and more pungent than the Indian.

CUBEB

Piper cubeba

Cubebs are the fruit of a tropical vine of the pepper family native to Java and other Indonesian islands. They were cultivated in Java from the 16th century and for 200 years cubebs were a popular substitute for black pepper in Europe. By the 19th century they had become almost unobtainable. Cubebs are now scarcely known in the West, but there is a revival of interest in them among spice aficionados.

PARTS USED

Immature fruits.

BUYING AND STORING

Cubebs are not easy to find, except from some spice merchants. Buy sparingly: although they keep their aromatic properties well, they are only used in small amounts. Stored whole in an airtight container they will keep for 2 years or more. Grind as needed.

HARVESTING

Cubebs are harvested green and sun-dried to a deep brown-black.

Culinary uses

Cubebs, also known as Java pepper and tailed pepper, are used locally in Indonesian cuisine and to a lesser extent in Sri Lanka, where they are also grown. They were traded from the 7th century by Arab merchants and formerly had a role in Arab cooking, one that persists mainly in their presence in the Moroccan spice mixture ras el hanout. Cubebs are used to flavor North African lamb or mutton tagines, and as a substitute for allspice in long-cooked stews. Cubebs are best suited to meat and vegetable dishes.

Cubebs are sometimes confused with the Ashanti pepper, *P. guineense*, an African species, and the Benin pepper, *P. clusii* – these also have stems and are often called false cubebs.

Combines well with bay, cardamom, cinnamon, curry leaf, rosemary, sage, thyme, turmeric.

Whole fruits

Cubebs are furrowed and wrinkled, slightly larger than peppercorns, and have a short, straight tail. Some berries contain a single seed, others are hollow.

Young or spring ginger

Pale young ginger with a translucent skin is sometimes found in Asian markets in spring. The flesh is creamy-white and crisp, the tips pink. It has a clean fragrance and tastes of ginger, but without a bite. Stir-fry with vegetables or cook lightly with seafood.

Pickled ginger

In Japan, knobs of ginger are pickled in sweet vinegar and served in wafer-thin slices with sushi as a digestive condiment, called gari. The taste is quite mild and pickling turns the ginger pink.

Beni-shoga is shredded ginger, dyed to a striking red by pickling and by being preserved with perilla leaves. More pungent than gari, it is good with crab and other seafood.

Preserved ginger

Ginger in syrup and crystallized ginger can be eaten as sweetmeats on their own or used as flavorings for sweet sauces, ice cream, cakes, and tarts.

Mioga ginger

The Japanese and Koreans share an enthusiasm for the mildly flavored young shoots and buds of mioga ginger, *Z. mioga*. They are sliced and used to flavor soups, tofu, salads, vinegared dishes, and pickles to accompany grilled foods.

FRESH MIOGA BUDS
Mioga buds are gathered in spring. They are fragrantly herbal rather than hot, and have a delicate, crunchy texture.

GINGER IN SYRUP
Knobs of young ginger are poached several times in a dense syrup so that the syrup penetrates the flesh. It is sometimes called stem ginger because both stems and rhizomes are used.

CRYSTALLIZED GINGER
To make this lightly pungent sweetmeat, knobs of young ginger are cooked in a thick syrup, air-dried, and rolled in sugar.

ALLSPICE

Pimenta dioica

TASTING NOTES

Allspice has a pleasantly warm, fragrant aroma. The name reflects the pungent taste, which resembles a peppery compound of cloves, cinnamon, and nutmeg or mace. Most of the flavor is in the shell rather than in the seeds it contains.

Allspice is native to the West Indies and tropical Central America. Columbus found it growing in the Caribbean islands and thought he had found the pepper he was looking for, hence allspice's Spanish name *pimienta* (pepper), which was anglicized as pimento. That name was later altered to Jamaica pepper because most of the crop, and certainly the best quality, came and still comes from that island. Allspice is the only important spice that still comes almost exclusively from its region of origin – which also makes it the only one grown almost exclusively in the New World.

PARTS USED

Dried berries.

BUYING AND STORING

Allspice can be bought whole or ground. Whole berries, which look like large, brown peppercorns, are infinitely preferable; they crush easily if you need just a little allspice, and they keep in an airtight jar almost indefinitely.

Whole dried berries

Jamaican allspice has the highest level of the essential oil that determines the taste. One of the main components of the oil is eugenol, which is also the principal flavoring element of cloves.

GROUND BERRIES
Ground allspice can lose its strength rather quickly.

HARVESTING

In Jamaica, berries are mostly harvested from trees cultivated in plantations. They are hand-picked when full size but still green. After a few days' sweating they are dried on black concrete platforms for up to a week. As they dry the berries turn red-brown. When dry – determined by the seeds rattling inside the shell – they are winnowed and graded by size. Larger, inferior, wild berries are still gathered in the rainforests of Mexico and Guatemala.

Culinary uses

Long before the discovery of the Americas, the people of the islands used allspice to preserve meat and fish. The Spaniards learned from them and used allspice in escabeches and other preserving liquids. In Jamaica, it is still an important ingredient in jerk seasoning pastes that are rubbed onto chicken, meat, or fish for grilling. It is also used extensively, crushed rather than ground, in breakfast breads, soups, stews, and curries. In the Middle East, allspice is used to season roasted meats. It is used in pilafs and goes into some Indian curries. In Europe, allspice is either used whole, as a pickling or mulling spice, or ground, to give a gentle, warm flavor to cakes, desserts, preserves, and fruit pies. Allspice enhances the flavor of pineapple, plums, black currants, and apples.

Most of the world's crop goes to the food industry for use in commercial ketchups and other sauces, as well as sausages, meat pies, Scandinavian pickled herrings, and sauerkraut. **Essential to** jerk spice mixtures. **Good with** eggplant, most fruit, pumpkins and other squashes, sweet potatoes and other root vegetables. **Combines well with** chili, cloves, coriander, garlic, ginger, mace, mustard, pepper, rosemary, thyme.

Sweet baking spice
Ground together, allspice berries, coriander seeds, cloves, mace, nutmeg, and cinnamon make up the sweet baking spice that is called mixed spice in Britain.

CLOVES
Syzyium aromaticum

TASTING NOTES

The aroma of cloves is assertive and warm, with notes of pepper and camphor. The taste is fruity but also sharp, hot, and bitter; it leaves a numbing sensation in the mouth. As in allspice, eugenol in the essential oil is mainly responsible for the characteristic taste.

PARTS USED

Dried flowerbuds.

BUYING AND STORING

Whole cloves vary greatly in size and appearance, but should be clean and intact. Good cloves exude a small amount of oil if pressed with a fingernail. They will keep for a year in an airtight jar. They are hard and must be ground in an electric mill. Ground cloves should be dark brown; lighter, gritty powders are likely to be mostly made from flower stems, which contain less of the volatile oil. The powder loses its strength quite quickly.

HARVESTING

Clove buds appear in small clusters, twice a year, from July to September and November to January. They are picked before flowering, when they are mature but only just turning pink at the base. Drying in the sun on woven mats, they lose most of their weight and turn reddish to dark brown.

The clove tree is a small, tropical evergreen with fragrant leaves. Its crimson flowers seldom develop, as unopened flowerbuds constitute the spice. Native to the Moluccas, volcanic islands now part of Indonesia, cloves reached Europe overland through Alexandria in Roman times. The Spice Islands were conquered by the Portuguese and then the Dutch, who harshly defended their monopoly until, in 1772, a French official smuggled seedlings to Ile-de-France (Mauritius). These days Zanzibar, Madagascar, and Pemba in Tanzania are the main exporters; Indonesia uses nearly all its vast production itself.

GROUND CLOVES
Ground cloves contribute their assertive warmth to most masalas and curry powders, to five-spice powder, berbere, and baharat.

Whole cloves
Good-quality cloves have reddish-brown stems and a lighter crown. They are rough to the touch and should snap cleanly.

Culinary uses

Cloves must be used sparingly, for they easily overpower other spices. They are equally good with sweet and savory foods. They go into baked goods, desserts, syrups, and preserves almost everywhere. In Europe, cloves are used as a pickling or mulling spice. The French press a single clove into an onion to flavor a stew, stock, or sauce; the Dutch use them more liberally in cheese and the English often too liberally in apple pie. In Germany, they are found in spiced breads, in the US in ham glazed with brown sugar. The candied walnuts of Turin have a clove stuck into one end. In the Middle East and North Africa, cloves go into spice blends used to flavor meat dishes or rice, often in combination with cinnamon and cardamom. In much of Asia, they appear in curry powders. In India, they are essential to garam masala, in China to five-spice powder, in France to quatre épices (with black pepper, nutmeg, and dried ginger). In Indonesia, cloves are mixed with tobacco for the very popular kretek cigarettes, which crackle as they burn and have a unique aroma.

Essential to quatre épices, five-spice powder, garam masala.

Good with apples, beets, red cabbage, carrots, chocolate, ham, onions, oranges, pork, pumpkin and other squashes, sweet potatoes.

Combines well with allspice, bay, cardamom, cinnamon, chili, coriander, curry leaves, fennel, ginger, mace, nutmeg, tamarind.

Five-spice powder

This Chinese blend of cloves, star anise, cassia, fennel seed, and Sichuan pepper goes well with chicken, duck, and pork.

MUSTARD

Brassica species

Black mustard, *B. nigra*, and white or yellow, *B. alba*, are native to southern Europe and western Asia, brown, *B. juncea*, to India. White mustard has long been naturalized in Europe and North America. The Romans, who made prepared mustard, introduced the plant to England. In medieval Europe, mustard was the one spice ordinary people could afford. The French started to add other ingredients in the 18th century, while the English refined the powder by removing the husks before grinding the kernels.

Culinary uses

In Western cooking, whole white mustard seeds are used primarily as a pickling and preserving spice, and in marinades.

Brown seeds (known as rai) have increasingly taken the place of black in much Indian cooking. In the south whole seeds are dry-roasted or tossed in hot oil or ghee to bring out an attractive nutty flavor. The dishes are not pungent because the hot oil does not activate myrosinase. In Bengal, ground raw seed is used in pastes for curries, especially fish in mustard sauce. Mustard oil –

viscous, deep golden and pungent – is widely used as a cooking oil; its piquant flavor adds to the distinctive taste of many Indian dishes. It is widely used as a cooking oil, most of all in Bengal, where it is heated to smoke point to reduce the smell, then cooled before use. Its piquant flavor contributes to the distinctive taste of many Indian dishes.

Shredded leaves make a pleasant garnish for root vegetables, and potato and tomato salads. In Vietnam, leaves are used to wrap stuffings of pork, shrimp, and herbs.

AMERICAN MUSTARD

ENGLISH MUSTARD

MOUTARDE AU CASSIS

TARRAGON MUSTARD

Prepared mustards

To prepare blended mustards, the seeds are soaked in water to activate the enzyme myrosinase; once the required heat has been achieved the enzyme's activity is stopped. The resulting flavor is determined largely by the acidic liquid used – vinegar gives a mild tang, wine or verjuice a more spicy pungency, beer a real heat. Water gives the sharpest, hottest taste, but will not stop the enzyme's activity and therefore does not make a stable mustard. Prepared mustards are best stored at room temperature even when opened; they will keep for 2–3 months, but they may dry out a little and will steadily lose their flavor.

French mustards are made in three forms. Bordeaux, although brown, is made from white seed and contains sugar and herbs. Dijon, made from brown seed and white wine or verjuice is paler and stronger. Meaux made from crushed and ground grains has a bite followed by mouth-filling roundness.

In Germany, Bavarian mustard is of the Bordeaux type, but Düsseldorf mustard is a pungent version of Dijon. Mild and runny American mustard is made from white mustard, with rather too much turmeric. English mustard powder is made up with cold water, then left for about 10 minutes to develop its clean and pungent taste. Once made up it will not keep.

These mustards are mainly used as a condiment in or with meat dishes or as a tracklement with cold meats. They are good in many cold sauces, in dressings for salads and to accompany cheese dishes. Sweet mustards make good glazes for meat and chicken.

Essential to panch phoron, sambhar powder.

Good with roast and grilled beef, cabbage, strong cheeses, chicken, curries, dals, fish and seafood, cold meats, rabbit, sausages.

Combines well with bay, chili, coriander, cumin, dill, fennel, fenugreek, garlic, honey, nigella, parsley, pepper, tarragon, turmeric.

MUSTARD OIL
Mustard oil is easier to digest after brief exposure to a very high temperature.

WHOLE SEEDS
Mustard's pungent taste is determined by an enzyme, myrosinase, which is activated by water.

CHILI PEPPERS
Capsicum species

Chili peppers range in taste from mild and tingling to explosively hot. The fruits of *C. frutescens* are generally hotter than those of *C. annuum*, and those of *C. chinense* are hottest of all. Large, fleshy varieties tend to be milder than small, thin-skinned peppers.

PARTS USED

Fresh and dried fruits. Immature chilies are green; they ripen to yellow, orange, red, brown, or purple, and may be used fresh or dried.

BUYING AND STORING

All fresh chilies should be shiny, smooth-skinned, and firm to the touch. They keep in the refrigerator vegetable crisper for a week or more. They can be blanched and frozen, but if frozen raw most lose their flavor and piquancy. Dried chilies vary in appearance according to the variety. A specialist merchant will tell you the country of origin, the type, flavor characteristics, and heat level. Dried chilies keep almost indefinitely in an airtight container.

HARVESTING

Most chilies are grown as annuals. Green chilies are picked 3 months after planting; varieties normally used ripe are left longer on the plant. Chilies may be dried in the sun or artificially.

Native to Central and South America and the Caribbean islands, chili peppers (or chile or hot peppers) have been cultivated there for thousands of years. Columbus took plants back to Spain, and the Spaniards named them *pimiento* (pepper) because of their pungency. Capsicum fruits are still called peppers even though they are not related to the pepper vine. Today chili peppers are the biggest spice crop; hundreds of different varieties are grown in all tropical regions and eaten daily by about a quarter of the world's population.

Whole fresh chili peppers
Chilies come in many colors, shapes, and sizes; they can be as tiny as a young pea or as long as 12in (30cm). Many of them stimulate the appetite not only with pungency but with fruity, floral, smoky, nutty, tobacco, or licorice flavors.

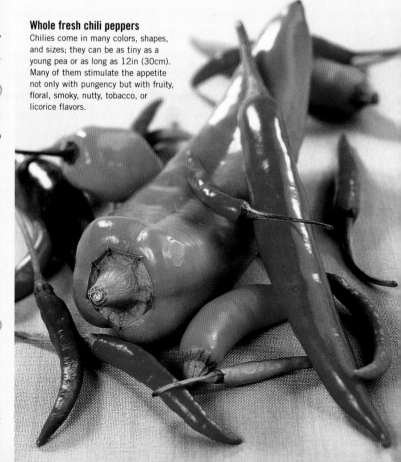

Culinary uses

Chili peppers are an excellent source of vitamins A and C, and provide that added benefit to the millions of people who eat them as a cheap means of pepping up a bland and unvarying diet. Chilies are used extensively in their native region, throughout Asia, in Africa, and in the American southwest. India is the largest producer and consumer of chilies, fresh green or dried red (which are usually ground), and each region uses its local varieties.

Mexican cooking makes the most sophisticated use of chili peppers, both fresh and dried.

The pungent bite of chilies is due to the presence of capsaicin in their seeds, white fleshy parts, and skin. The capsaicin content depends on the variety of chili pepper and its degree of ripeness; removing seeds and veins will reduce the heat of the chili. Capsaicin stimulates the digestive process and the circulation, which induces perspiration and has a cooling effect on the body.

Essential to berbere, chili powder (which is actually a combination of spices), curry powders and pastes, harissa, jerk seasoning, kimchi, moles, nam prik, pipián, romesco sauce, sambals.
Combines well with most spices, bay, coriander, rau ram, coconut milk, lemon and lime juice.

The heat of chili peppers is rated on a scale of 1–10, from 1 for mild peppers to 10 for extremely hot scotch bonnets.

GROUND HOT CHILI
Ground chili is made from dried hot red chilies. Heat rather than flavor is often the characteristic of these products, **5–9/10** on the heat scale, depending on the variety.

DRIED CHILI OR PEPPER FLAKES
Produced from mild to moderately hot chili peppers, **2–5/10**, these are often used as a table condiment in Hungary, Turkey, and the Middle East. Hotter chili flakes are used as a condiment in Korea and Japan.

CHILI THREADS
Red chili peppers are an essential Korean ingredient. Very fine chili threads are used as a garnish.

WHOLE DRIED CHILI PEPPERS
Drying changes the flavors of chilies. Similarly, the taste of green, immature chilies alters as they ripen and redden.

Chili products

Ground chili, chili pastes, sauces, and oils are produced worldwide. Good-quality ground chili smells fruity, earthy, and pungent and contains traces of natural oils that will stain the fingers slightly. A light orange color indicates the inclusion of a high proportion of seeds, which makes for a sharper taste. Thin, pungent sauces are labeled salsa picante or hot pepper sauce; some combine chilies with astringent ingredients such as limes or tamarind. Thick sauces, based on tomatoes, onions, garlic, and herbs, may be mild or hot and are often sweetened. Indonesian sambals and Thai chili jam are among the hottest. The Chinese use soy sauce, black beans, ginger, and garlic to create medium to hot sauces. Korean gochu-jang is a sticky condiment made with chilies, soybean paste, and rice flour.

CHILI POWDER
This blend of ground chili, cumin, dried oregano, paprika, and garlic powder is used to flavor chile con carne and other southwestern dishes. **1–3/10**

CHILI OIL
Seasoning oil made with dried red chilies is available commercially, but it is easy to make your own: fill one-third of a bottle with dried chili peppers, top up with sunflower oil, close tightly, and leave for 1 month. In Sichuan, crushed dried chilies are added to very hot oil, left to cool for several hours, then strained to produce a bright red oil, used in many cold sauces and on its own as a dip.

YELLOW GROUND CHILI
The color of ground chilies ranges from yellow to red and mahogany. Yellow ground chili is used in South America; it can be mild or hot.

CAYENNE OR RED PEPPER
The most common ground chili, cayenne is made from small, ripe chili peppers grown worldwide. The flavour is tart, slightly smoky, and intensely pungent. **8/10**

THIN SAUCES

Thin sauces are made from crushed chilies blended with spices and vinegar to produce fiery liquids. Tabasco sauce is the best-known example.

CHILI SAUCES

Chili sauces are made in most regions where chili peppers are grown. The simplest types are made from whole chilies preserved in brine or vinegar. Thick sauces, which may be cooked or made from raw ingredients, are used as dips and condiments.

CHILI JAM AND SAMBAL

Chili pastes and thick sauces enliven stir-fries and slow-cooked dishes. At the end of this book are recipes for chili jam and sambals.

Mexico

In Mexico, fresh and dried versions of a chili pepper often have different names. Specific chilies are required for specific dishes; using the wrong one can alter the balance of flavors. Large, fleshy poblanos are used as a vegetable, often stuffed; jalapeños and serranos appear in salsas, stuffings, and pickles; dried anchos and pasillas are often ground to thicken a sauce. When used fresh, green chili peppers tend to be preferred, and they are often charred and peeled before being used.

Serrano *C. annuum*

Mid-green, cylindrical, crisp-textured, with a concentrated, fresh, grassy flavor and very pungent seeds and veins. It ripens to bright red. Commonly used in sauces. **6–7/10**

Jalapeño *C. annuum*

Bright green, some with dark patches, torpedo-shaped, quite fat with crisp, thick flesh. Sometimes roasted and peeled. Jalapeños have a light flavor and are medium-hot. Red and fully ripe they are sweeter and less hot. Also sold canned en escabeche (pickled) and widely used as a table condiment. **5–6/10**

Habanero *C. chinense*

Lantern-shaped, mid-green ripening to yellow, orange, and deep red, thin-fleshed, and fruity. Mostly used in Yucatán, raw or roasted, to flavor beans and sauces. For a hot sauce, blend roasted habaneros with salt and lime juice. **10/10**

Chilaca *C. annuum*

Thin, deep red and shiny, with vertical ridges. The deep flavor has a hint of licorice. Roasted and peeled, they are used in vegetable dishes, with cheese, and in sauces. Sometimes available pickled. **6–7/10**

OTHER CHILI PEPPERS

Mulato (*C. annuum*) is similar to ancho, but chocolate brown; the taste is full-bodied, sweeter than ancho, with notes of dried cherries, and mild to medium-hot. Mostly toasted and ground for sauces. **3–5/10**

De arból (*C. annuum*) is seldom found fresh; it remains bright red when dried. Slender, curved, and pointed, with thin flesh and a smooth skin, it is searingly hot and

has a somewhat tannic flavor. Soaked and then puréed, de arbóls are used in stews and as a table sauce. **8/10**

Poblano (*C. annuum*) is dark green and shiny, with a ridge around the base of the stem. The shape is triangular and tapering, and the flesh is thick. Roasted and peeled, poblanos are stuffed or fried. They pair well with corn and tomatoes, and have a rich flavor. **3–4/10**

Pasilla (*C. annuum*) is the dried chilaca, slender, wrinkled, and almost black. It has an astringent yet rich flavor with herby notes that is complex and long-lasting. Toasted and ground it is used in table sauces or in cooked sauces for fish. **6–7/10**

Güero (*C. annuum*) is pale yellow, smooth, long, and pointed, with thin flesh. The taste is lightly floral, mild to medium-hot. Güeros are used fresh in salsas and moles. **4–5/10**

Cascabel *c. annuum*

This is round and brown-red, with a smooth, translucent skin; the seeds rattle when you shake it. It has a lightly acidic, smoky flavor and is agreeably nutty after toasting. Moderately hot, it is toasted and blended with tomatoes or tomatillos to make a salsa, and crumbled in stews. **4–5/10**

Chipotle *c. annuum*

The smoke-dried jalapeño. Tan to coffee-colored, wrinkled, leathery, it has a smoky, sweet, chocolate smell and taste. Often used whole to flavor soups and stews. Soaked and puréed, it goes into sauces. Available canned in a light pickle for use as a condiment. **5–6/10**

Ancho *c. annuum*

This is a dried poblano. Deep red-brown, wrinkled, fruity, and sweet with rich flavors of tobacco, prune, and raisin, and slightly hot. Anchos are toasted and ground for sauces, or can be stuffed. Also available as powder and blocks of paste. The most popular dried chili pepper. **3–4/10**

Guajillo *c. annuum*

This is long and slender, with a blunt point; maroon with brown tones and a smooth, tough skin, it has high acidity, giving a tangy, pleasantly sharp taste. It is soaked and blended for enchilada sauces or crumbled into stews. It colors foods well. **4/10**

Southwest US and Caribbean

West Indians tend to prefer hot chili peppers for marinades, relishes, and stews.
Early hot sauces mixed chilies and cassava juice; now garlic, onion, and other spices
give depth to Caribbean chili sauces. In the American southwest, Mexican varieties
are used in Mexican-inspired dishes, but the local New Mexican chili, used green,
red, and dried, is mild. These chilies are hung out to dry in colorful ristras; once
dried they are often ground and sold as Chimayo chili powder or chile colorado.

Jamaican hot *C. chinense*

Bright red and squat with thin flesh, this
tastes sweet and very hot. Use in salsas,
pickles, and curries. **9/10**

New Mexico *C. annuum*

Bright green or a deep, intense red, this has a sweet,
earthy flavor. It is roasted and peeled, and keeps well if
frozen after roasting. Green is good in guacamole, tacos,
and tamales; red goes into sauces, soups, and chutneys.
Dried, this has rich, dried-fruit flavors. It is used
for red chili sauce and other relishes. **2–3/10**

Scotch bonnet *C. chinense*

Yellow-green to orange-red, similar in appearance to
the closely related habanero but with a wrinkled top
and flattened base. Very hot and with a deep, fruity,
smoky flavor. Used in many Caribbean hot
sauces and in jerk seasoning. **10/10**

Tabasco *C. frutescens*

Thin-fleshed and yellow, turning orange or red when
ripe, this has a sharp, biting taste with a hint
of celery. It is mostly used for Tabasco sauce. **8/10**

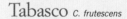

Latin America

Called ají, chili peppers are much used in the Andean countries as a flavoring and as a condiment; a bowl of uchu llajawa – a fiery salsa of hot chilies and quillquiña (a local "cilantro") – is always on the table. Many varieties have only local names; some are mild, some bitter, particularly the yellow ones, and some dried chilies have rich flavors of raisin and prune. Chilies are also important in the cooking of Bahia in Brazil; elsewhere bottled chili sauce is more common.

Rocoto *C. pubescens*

Native to the Andes; plump and rounded, yellow to orange-red, rocotos are always used fresh in sauces and condiments, or as a vegetable, often stuffed with meat and cheese. **8–9/10**

Ají amarillo *C. baccatum*

Common in Peru, both fresh and dried, when it is called cusqueño. Pointed and hot with raisiny aromas, it is used with potatoes and other root vegetables, guinea pig (the local specialty), ceviche, and other seafood dishes. **7/10**

Mirasol *C. annuum*

This is popular in Peru and also found in Mexico, where the dried form is known as guajillo. Used green, yellow, or at its ripe, red-brown stage. Fruity and lively, it colors dishes well. Good with meats, beans, and vegetables. **5/10**

OTHER CHILI PEPPERS

Ají dulce (*C. annuum*) is sweet, mild, musky, and herbal-like. It is used extensively in Central America, Colombia, and Venezuela, especially with beans. **1/10**

Rocotillo (*C. chinense*) is a mild Andean chili pepper, bright red and squashed-looking, that is eaten as a condiment with corn, beans, root vegetables, and roast meats. **3–4/10**

Malagueta (*C. frutescens*) is pale or mid green, thin-fleshed, tapered, and tiny. It is native to Bahia in Brazil and widely used in Afro-Brazilian cooking and as a table condiment. Malagueta is also the name given in Portugal to small hot chilies pickled in vinegar. **8/10**

Asia

Asian chili peppers are even harder to pinpoint by name than Latin American ones. They are usually distinguished by types: large red and green ones, which are roasted and used in dips and sauces in Southeast Asia; medium-sized, shiny-skinned chilies, moderately hot, used in Indonesian and Malay cooking; and more pungent varieties for Thai and Indian curries. Japanese santakas and hontakas resemble cayennes.

Thai *C. annuum*

Used fresh and dried, these are slender, and dark green or bright red, with meaty flesh and lingering heat. Add whole to curries and stir-fries or chop for pastes and dips. **8/10**

Korean *C. annuum*

The bright green, curved, Korean chili pepper is related to the Thai. Fresh ones are cooked in fish, meat, and vegetable stews, in stir-fries, or stuffed and fried. **6–7/10**

Bird *C. frutescens*

The tiny green, orange, and red chilies are all used, often whole, to give a "finishing" flavor to a dish. They are fiercely hot. **9/10**

Kashmir *C. annuum*

Grown not only in Kashmir but in other parts of India, this is deep red and has sweet notes yet a distinct bite. In India, it is called lal mirch. **7/10**

Europe

A few chili peppers are specific to Europe, although many more are used in imported dishes. Hungary, Spain, and Portugal are the countries where local chilies are most used, and they are usually only mildly hot.

Peperoncino *C. annuum*

These are slender, wrinkled, and often curved, with thin flesh. Used fresh, green or red, in pickles and tomato-based dishes, the flavor is sweetish. **1–4/10**

Guindilla *C. annuum*

Brick-red and smooth, this long, tapering Spanish chili is used dried. Large pieces are soaked and added to a dish for extra piquancy; remove before serving. **5/10**

Banana *C. annuum*

Yellow-green ripening to red, curved, with a waxy skin, this mild chili is related to the hotter Hungarian wax. Use fresh in salads, stews, roasted whole, with legumes or potatoes, pickled, and as a garnish. **1/10**

Ñora *C. annuum*

This is mild and pleasantly earthy. It is soaked and used to flavor rice dishes and stews. Ñoras are essential to romesco sauce and for sweet paprika. The larger, bell-shaped choricero is similar and, as its name suggests, is used to flavor chorizo and other meat products. **1–2/10**

OTHER CHILI PEPPERS

Cherry (*C. annuum*) is orange to deep red when fresh, mahogany when dried, with a thick flesh and lots of seeds. It has a fruity flavor and ranges from mild to medium-hot. It is often sold pickled. **1–5/10**

Peri peri (*C. annuum*) is the Portuguese name for small chili peppers. It crops up in those parts of the world colonized by the Portuguese. In Africa, it is used for the jindungo chili, which is similar to the bird chili. **9/10**

Piment d'Espelette (*C. annuum*) from the Basque country has an appellation contrôlée. Bright red, wide-shouldered, and tapering, it is sweetly fruity and mildly piquant. Available dried, whole or as a powder, and also as a purée or coulis. **3/10**

preparing spices

BRUISING, GRATING, SLICING, AND SHREDDING SPICES

Many spices need some preparation before being added to a dish or used in a spice blend or paste. Bruising, cutting, and grinding serve to release the volatile oils and perfume of a spice. Large, bruised pieces of a spice are intended only for flavoring and should be removed before a dish is served. Mild spices are sometimes cut into bite-sized pieces and eaten as part of the dish; otherwise, spices should be grated, finely sliced, or shredded.

Bruising spices

Soft-textured fresh spices such as lemon grass, ginger, galangal, aromatic ginger, and zedoary (white turmeric) are often bruised before cooking to release their flavors, then added whole for later removal.

1 ▲ Remove the upper part of a lemon grass stalk (or peel a knob of the other spices).

2 ▶ Crush the lower part of the lemon grass stalk (or the peeled knob) using the back of a heavy knife or a wooden meat pounder.

Slicing and shredding spices

Some dishes require disks of fresh spices, while others call for spices to be shredded or chopped. The procedure for spices such as ginger, galangal, or zedoary (white turmeric) is given below. Lemon grass is cut into fine rings from the base, stopping when the texture becomes fibrous. Kaffir lime leaves should be shredded as fine as a needle if they are to be eaten.

 Peel as much fresh rhizome or root as you need, cutting off any woody or dry bits.

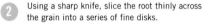 Using a sharp knife, slice the root thinly across the grain into a series of fine disks.

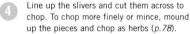 Stack the disks, press down firmly, and shred them into fine slivers.

Line up the slivers and cut them across to chop. To chop more finely or mince, mound up the pieces and chop as herbs (p.78).

DRY-ROASTING AND FRYING SPICES

Roasting whole spices in a dry frying pan is especially common in Indian cooking. The process intensifies the flavors and makes the spices easier to grind. Other dishes call for spices to be fried before other ingredients are added. Frying brings out the flavor, which is imparted to the oil. The aroma of fried spices permeates a dish more fully than that of raw spices, but once a liquid is added the amount of fragrance they release is reduced.

Dry-roasting spices

Some seed spices, notably mustard seeds, tend to jump about as they roast, so have a lid available to cover the pan. A tablespoon of spices will be ready in 2–3 minutes, whereas a large quantity can take up to 8–10 minutes to brown evenly. With large quantities, roast each spice separately.

1. ▲ Heat a heavy pan until it feels hot when you hold your hand over it.

2. ▶ With the pan over a medium heat, toss in the spices. Stir them or shake the pan constantly. Let the spices darken and smoke a little, and they will soon give off a heady aroma. If they are changing color too quickly, lower the heat and make sure they do not burn.

3. Pour the spices into a bowl and let cool before grinding them.

Dry-roasting in an oven or microwave

Dry-roasting in an oven ▶

Dry-roasting a large quantity of spices may be easier in an oven preheated to 500°F (250°C). Spread the spices on a baking sheet and roast in the oven until they darken and are aromatic, shaking and stirring from time to time. Let cool before grinding.

Frying spices

Prepare all the ingredients of a dish before frying its spices. Some spices are fried for only a few seconds, others for up to a minute. All will darken, and some, such as cardamom pods, will puff up. Remove the pan from the heat to add more ingredients, and stir quickly to prevent them from burning in the oil.

1 ▲ Pour a thin film of sunflower oil into a heavy frying pan and heat until you can see a faint haze rising over the pan.

2 ▶ Fry whole spices before ground ones, adding them in the order they appear in the recipe. Spices should sizzle when they hit the hot oil and brown almost instantly. Watch them closely to prevent burning.

GRINDING, CRUSHING, AND MAKING SPICE PASTES

Freshly ground or crushed spices are always more aromatic than spices bought ready-ground. You will soon appreciate the difference if you take the trouble to grind, say, a teaspoon of coriander seeds and put them to one side for an hour or two. Then grind another spoonful. Smell the older batch and then the freshly ground seeds – you will find that some of the aroma of the first batch has already dissipated.

Grinding spices

Some whole spices – allspice, cinnamon, and cloves, for example – are aromatic, but most need to be crushed or ground to release their aroma. A blender can be used for a large quantity, but most spices are too hard to grind evenly in a food processor.

Using a mortar and pestle ▷
Choose a mortar that is deep, sturdy, and roughly textured, because many spices are very hard and considerable force is needed to grind them by hand.

Using an electric mill
Most spices can be ground in a spice mill, or coffee grinder kept specially for the purpose, although a few, such as anardana (see p.111), are too sticky.

Crushing spices

Some spices need only to be crushed, rather than pulverized to a powder. A mortar and pestle works well because you can easily see and control how much the spice is broken up – and you can enjoy its fragrance at the same time.

Using a rolling pin ▷
Put the spice in a plastic bag, spread out the seeds on a hard surface, then crush firmly with a rolling pin.

Making spice pastes

Spice pastes are made by crushing fresh spices (such as garlic, ginger, galangal, or zedoary) together with dry spices or herbs and sometimes a little liquid. The technique is widely used in India and Southeast Asia, and in Mexico. Use a mortar and pestle or the small bowl of a food processor.

1 ▶ If using any dry spices, grind them first, either in the mortar or in an electric mill.

2 ▼ Crush the garlic or ginger, then work in the ground spices, and finally the liquid if needed.

FRESH CHILI PEPPERS

Chili peppers come in many shapes, colors, and sizes, and the flavor changes from the young, green state to the mature, red or red-brown state. When chilies are dried, their flavor changes again. Often fresh chili peppers are used whole or sliced in a recipe, but sometimes they benefit from seeding or roasting, especially if they have tough skins.

Roasting fresh chili peppers

Most chilies can be used without peeling, but some are roasted and peeled because the skin is tough or because peeling will improve the texture and give a pleasant charred flavor. Small chilies can be roasted on a preheated dry griddle or heavy frying pan. Turn them until they darken and soften.

1 Hold large chilies directly over a gas flame, turning from time to time so that they are charred evenly and the flesh doesn't burn. Or, lay them on a grill that rests above an electric burner. Alternatively, hold them close to the preheated element of the broiler and turn them as they blister and blacken.

2 ▲Once they are evenly charred, put the chilies into a plastic bag or a bowl covered with plastic wrap and let sweat for 10–15 minutes.

3 ▶Carefully peel off the skin and rinse. Dry the chilies on paper towel.

Freezing chili peppers

Fresh chilies can be frozen after roasting. There is no need to peel them because the skin will come off when the chilies have thawed.

Freezing unroasted chili peppers ▷
Blanch unroasted chilies with stems intact for 3 minutes, then drain in a colander. Let cool completely, place in a plastic bag, and freeze.

Removing seeds and veins from fresh chili peppers

Capsaicin, the pungent principle that gives chilies their heat, is present in varying degrees in the seeds, white veins, and skin. Capsaicin can sting the skin and eyes (*see below*). Removing seeds and veins before cooking reduces the heat of a dish.

1 Cut off and remove the stems, and slice each of the chilies in half.

2 ◀ Cut out the veins and scrape out all the seeds, then rinse.

CAUTION

- If you are not used to handling chilies or have any cuts or a sensitive skin, wear thin rubber or plastic gloves to protect against the capsaicin.

- Remember that the seeds and veins are the hottest part of chilies. Avoid rubbing your eyes – if you do, rinse them at once with cold water.

- When you have finished handling chilies, use soapy water to wash your hands thoroughly, as well as the work surface and any utensils.

- If your hands do suffer chili burn, put them in a bowl of cold water or light vegetable oil.

- If you burn your mouth when eating a chili, a drink of water will make it worse. Instead, chew a piece of bread or try yogurt or milk.

DRIED CHILI PEPPERS

Large dried chili peppers, widely used in the cooking of Mexico and the southwestern US, are usually toasted, then soaked and puréed before use in a sauce. Toasting enhances their flavor; for a milder dish, the chilies are just soaked. In Mexico, smaller varieties of dried chilies are frequently ground or puréed straight into a sauce. Asian cooks are more likely to toast small dried chilies before grinding them.

Removing seeds and veins from dried chili peppers

As with fresh chilies, removing the seeds and veins from dried chilies before use reduces the heat of the dish. Seeds and veins are best removed before toasting, so that the chilies are ready for soaking or grinding immediately after they have been toasted.

Shaking out seeds ▷
Wipe the chilies clean, then either tear them apart or break off the stems and shake out the seeds.

Toasting dried chili peppers

Toasted dried chilies darken in color, blister, and crackle as they release their aroma. Don't let them scorch or they will taste acrid and bitter. Once toasted they are ready for soaking or grinding.

◁ Using a griddle
Place cleaned dried chilies on a preheated griddle or heavy frying pan for 1–2 minutes, turning them so that they don't burn. Alternatively, toast them for 2–3 minutes in an oven preheated to 500°F (250°C).

Soaking dried chili peppers

If you need small, soaked dried chilies for an Asian spice paste, tear them into pieces and add to water. They should be ready for use in 15 minutes.

1 ▲ Place toasted or cleaned, dried chilies in a bowl and cover with almost-boiling water. Keep the chilies submerged by setting a saucer or plate on top of them and let soak for 15 minutes or until soft – large, thick ones may need longer.

2 ▶ Rub the soft chilies through a wire strainer to remove the tough skins, then make a sauce by blending them with other ingredients and

Grinding dried chili peppers

Wipe the chilies clean, remove the stems, and tear the skins into pieces. Retain the seeds and veins if you need additional heat in the dish; otherwise remove them before grinding.

Using an electric mill ▶
Dried chilies can be ground to a fine consistency in an electric spice mill or coffee grinder. Better results

INDEX

The index is divided into two parts
Common and botanical names (*p.189*)
and General (*191*).

Common and botanical names

(a reference to a recipe indicates that the
ingredient is essential to that recipe)

A

achiote 142–43
Aframomum spp. 130
agastache 37
Agastache spp. 37
ají 175
ajowan 147
alligator pepper 153
Allium sativum 48
Allium schoenoprasum 50
Allium tuberosum 51
allspice 162–63
Aloysia citriodora 34
Alpinia spp. 118–19
amchoor 113
Amomum melegueta 153
Amomum spp. 130
amsul 112
anardana 110–11
ancho chili pepper 173
Anethum graveolens 42–43
anise (seed) 124
anise hyssop 37
annatto 142–43
Anthriscus cerefolium 38–39
Apium graveolens 52
Armoracia rusticana 72–73
Artemisia dracunculoides 41
Artemisia dracunculus 40–41
Artemisia vulgaris 75
arugula 68–69
asafetida 158
asem 107
Ashanti pepper 152
avocado leaf 155

B

bai gaprow 25
bai horopa 25
balm 32, 33
banana chili pepper 177
barberry 109
basil 22-25
bay 26–27
bee balm 32
Benin pepper 152
Berberis vulgaris 109
bergamot 32
betel pepper 154
bird chili pepper 176
bitter orange 120–21
Bixa orellana 142–43
black cardamom 130
black mangosteen 112
black mint 21
black onion seed 89
Bohnenkraut 65
borage 16
Borago officinalis 16
Brassica spp. 166–67
Bunias orientalis 69
Bunium persicum 135
burnet 17

C

Calendula officinalis 20–21
capers 145
Capparis spp. 145
Capsicum annuum spp. 104–105
Capsicum baccatum 175
Capsicum chinense 168, 172, 174–75
Capsicum frutescens 168, 175–76
Capsicum pubescens 175
Capsicum spp.168–177
caraway 136–37
cardamom 128–130
carom 147
cascabel 173
Carum carvi 136–37
cassia 96–97
céleri bâtard 53
celery 52
chaa phluu 154
Chenopodium ambrosioides 74
cherry chili pepper 177
chervil 38–39
chicory 55
chilaca 172
chili peppers 168–77
Chinese celery 52
Chinese chives 51
Chinese parsley 66–67

chipotle chili pepper 173
chives 50
choricero chili pepper 177
Cichorium intybus 55
cilantro 66–67
Cinnamomum spp. 94–97
cinnamon 94–95
citron 120
citrus 120–21
Citrus hystrix 116–17
Citrus spp. 120–21
claytonia 15
Claytonia perfoliata 15
cloves 164–65
coriander (seed) 98–99
Coriandrum sativum (herb) 66–67
Coriandrum sativum (spice) 98–99
Crocus sativus 126–27
Cryptotaenia japonica 19
cubeb 152
cumin 134–35
Cuminum cyminum 134–35
Curcuma longa 132–33
Curcuma spp. 131
curry leaf 144
cusqueño chili pepper 175
Cymbopogon citratus 114–15

D E

de arból chili pepper 173
dhana-jeera 98, 134
dill 42–43
Diplotaxis muralis 69
Elettaria cardamomum 128–29
epazote 74
Eruca vesicaria subsp. *sativa* 68–69
Eugenia polyantha 155
Eutrema wasabi 70–71

F

fagara 156
fennel 44–45
fenugreek 146
Ferula spp. 158
fish tamarind 112
flower pepper 156
Foeniculum vulgare 44–45
French marigold 21

G

galangal 118
Gänsekraut 75

GENERAL

ACKNOWLEDGMENTS

Author's acknowledgments
Thanks first to my husband, Paul Breman, who helped with research, and encouraged me constantly throughout the writing of the book. He also compiled the index.

Many friends generously provided information or samples from their own part of the world or their own area of expertise; thanks go to Lynda Brown, Vic Cherikoff, Nevin Halıcı, Ian Hemphill, Richard Hosking, Philip Iddison, Aglaia Kremezi, Myung Sook Lee, Maricel Presilla, Diny Schouten, Maria José Sevilla, Margaret Shaida, David Thompson, Yong Suk Willendrup, Paula Wolfert, and Sami Zubaida.

William Penzey of The Spice House in Milwaukee generously provided a wealth of spices and information; Dr P.S.S. Thampi of the Spices Board of India provided useful contacts in Kerala; Summa Navaratnam and N.M. Wickramasinghe helped on cinnamon production; Patricia Raymond of Aust & Hachmann gave help on vanilla; the Hungarian Trade Office and Foods from Spain on paprika and pimentón; Sarah Wain of West Dean Gardens took me through their impressive collection of chilies; Kevin Bateman of MSK provided samples of Kashmiri saffron and bourbon vanilla; Chris Seagon of Laurel Herb Farm provided herbs; Jason Stemm sent me statistics from the American Spice Trade Association, and A.C. Whitely of the Royal Horticultural Society and Dr Mark Nesbitt of the Royal Botanic Gardens at Kew helped me to identify golpar.

At Dorling Kindersley publisher Mary-Clare Jerram, art director Carole Ash, and their team conceived an exciting and ambitious book; Gillian Roberts has been an exemplary managing editor; Frank Ritter and Hugh Thompson have been painstaking and constructive in their editing; Toni Kay and Sara Robin have produced a handsome and imaginative design; and Dave King has produced lively and informative photographs of all the herbs and spices. My thanks go to all of them.

Publisher's acknowledgments
Dorling Kindersley would like to thank Marghie Gianni and Jo Gray for design assistance; Sarah Duncan for picture research; Jo Harris for research and styling; Nancy Campbell for research and sourcing items for photography; Jim Arbury for his splendid Hamburg parsley; Patty Penzey of The Spice House; Debbie Yakeley at Richters in Ontario; and all those who helped us in Florida, making it possible to photograph many fresh herbs and chilies when they were unobtainable in the UK – Linda Cunningham in Jacksonville and Maggie at Maggie's Herb Farm, Della and Tim Baldwin at Palm Valley Peppers, and Paul Figura.

All images © Dorling Kindersley
The Dorling Kindersley picture library contains over 2.5 million images, including travel photography, food, and drink. For more information, visit www.dkimages.com